The Souvenir Guide

to the

GETTYSBURG

National

Military

Park

James A. Gross

Andre B. Collins

Maps by James A. Gross   Photos by the Authors

Civil War Photos courtesy Library of Congress

and National Archives

Distributed by

302 York St.

Gettysburg, PA 17325-1996

AUTHOR'S NOTES

The purpose of this book is twofold. Its primary objective is to entertain the visitor while exploring the Gettysburg National Military Park.

The second objective is to make available to the visitor an easy to follow account of the battle with maps and photographs. Not everyone wishes to follow the battle in depth, but for those who do, this book certainly will be of value.

Dover, Penna.

J A Gross

April 1, 1971

A B Collins

No battle in American History surpasses in fame, and few military encounters excel in significance, the bloody Battle of Gettysburg.

Fourth Revised Edition

Distributed by

302 York St.
Gettysburg, PA 17325-1996

CONTENTS

LIST OF MAPS

Major General George Gordon Meade was born in Spain of American parents. He returned to this country with them and entered West Point in 1831. Graduating in 1835, Meade served in the Seminole Wars but resigned in 1836 for a career in civil engineering. He returned to the army in 1842 to fight in the Mexican War and again against the Seminoles.

In 1861 he was appointed Brigadier General and he commanded a Pennsylvania Brigade during the Peninsular Campaign where he was seriously wounded at **Frayser's farm.** He later moved up to command a division, then the V Corps and finally took command of the Army of the Potomac on June 28, 1863.

For being in command **for only three days,** Meade handled the army well at Gettysburg. He was severly censured for not pursuing Lee, but was later thanked officially by Congress for his service at Gettysburg. He retained command of the Army of the Potomac until the close of the war, being advanced to the rank of Major General in the regular army in 1864.

After the war Meade commanded first the Military Division of the Atlantic, next the Department of the East, and then the third military district of the South. In 1869 he resumed command to the Military Division of the Atlantic. He died from pneumonia in 1872 while commanding this post.

National Archives

Major General John Fulton Reynolds was born in Lancaster, Pennsylvania, only fifty miles from the point where he would meet his death. After graduation from West Point in 1841, Reynolds had various garrison duties until The Mexican War where he was cited numerous times for gallantry. After the Mexican War, he held various posts, including Commandant of Cadets at West Point.

At the outbreak of war, Reynolds commanded a regiment, later he commanded a brigade. During the Peninsular Campaign, he was captured at Gaines Mill. After six weeks in prison, he was exchanged for General Barksdale. It's ironic that both of these men should be killed in this same battle.

Considered to be second in command to Meade, Reynolds commanded the three Corps comprising the left wing of the army several days before Gettysburg. While leading his troops into action the first day at Gettysburg, Reynolds was shot from his horse and killed instantly. His body was taken to Lancaster where he was buried three days later.

General Robert E. Lee was born January 19, 1807, the fifth child of "Light-Horse Harry" Lee. Following graduation in 1829 at West Point, Lee joined General Winfield Scott's campaign which led to the capture of Mexico City.

In 1861, he became Colonel of his regiment, but upon the secession of his native Virginia he gave up his commission. He then offered his services to his state. Although opposed to disunion, he accepted command of the Virginia Army and subsequently Commander in Chief of Confederate forces. After a series of victories, Gettysburg became his first true defeat.

By 1864, the South's forces and supplies became exhausted. Lee managed to hold the battered army together until April, 1865. After the loss of Richmond, he surrendered to General Grant at Appomattox Courthouse on April 9, 1865.

Loved and respected by his men, he also commanded great respect from his opponents. His moral courage and military shrewdness left him above and beyond any commander of his day.

One of the sublimest statements in the history of warfare is his remark to General Pickett after the climatic charge of July 3. "This has been my fight and upon my shoulders rests the blame. . . . .Your men have done all that men could do. The fault is entirely my own." If Lee had a weakness, it was his excessive consideration for others.

He spent his last years as president of Washington College, the post he held at his death in 1870.

Lieutenant General James Longstreet was born in Edgefield, South Carolina on January 8, 1821 and was raised on a plantation in Georgia. After graduating from West Point in 1842, he served in the war in Mexico and was recognized twice for bravery. He resigned a Major's commission in June, 1861 and was appointed Confederate Brigadier General. When Lee divided his army into two Corps, he gave the first to Longstreet and the second to "Stonewall" Jackson.

National Archives

Longstreet's conduct at Gettysburg on the second and third day led to accusations after the war that his tardy execution of Lee's orders lost the battle for the South. Longstreet was a brave and determined fighter, however, many critics believe he was often too slow getting under way.

After the war, he became minister to Turkey and later U.S. Commissioner of the Pacific Railroad. He held the latter at the time of his death in 1904.

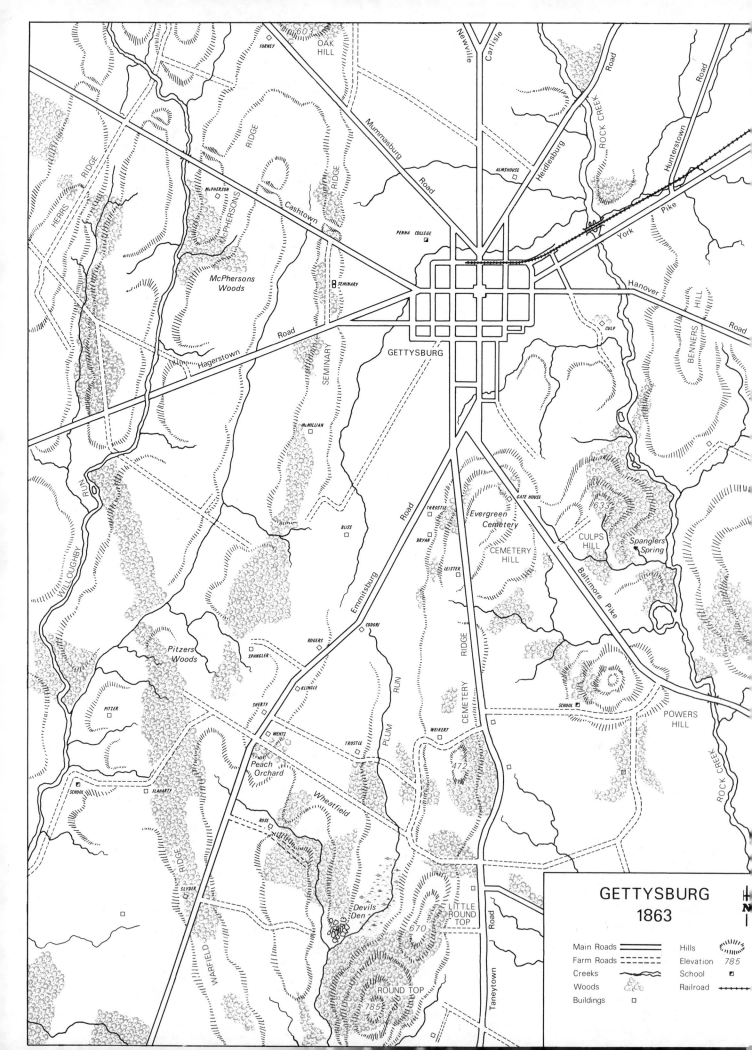

GETTYSBURG
1863

Main Roads
Farm Roads
Creeks
Woods
Buildings

Hills
Elevation   *785*
School
Railroad

BATTLEFIELD TOUR

The following 18-mile driving tour and associated map (Back Cover) is designed to guide and inform you of the many interesting areas and memorials in the National Military Park. The official route and stops are used in this tour but have been supplemented by additional points of interest. The tour may be started at any point along the route, but it should be started at the Visitors Center for a better understanding of the battle. Please follow the Auto Tour signs.

Located on Cemetery Ridge opposite the National Cemetery, the Visitors Center offers an excellent beginning for your visit to Gettysburg. The Electric Map orientation program is highly recommended before touring the battlefield. Nearby is the Cyclorama Center where a free film and a small museum introduces the visitor to the story of Gettysburg. Not to be missed is the Cyclorama, an immense oil painting 356 feet in circumference, depicting "Pickett's Charge" at its climax on the afternoon of July 3, 1863.

The National Military Park offers many opportunities to those who wish to tour the battlefield at their own pace. Several "Walking tours" are included and many side roads allow the visitor an opportunity to explore the many areas of interest not included in the official tour route.

To assist the visitor during the auto tour, recommended stops are marked in blue circles. Interesting landmarks and memorials are indicated in red numbers. The numbers as they appear on the map (Back Cover) are explained here.

The Gettysburg area offers many Civil War museums for visitors. Relics dating from the period are on display, including uniforms, weapons and ammunition. Several museums offer movies or maps to help the visitor further understand the importance of this battle.

Many family camping grounds and motels are located within several miles of the Park for the overnight visitor.

 McPhersons Ridge To your left, along the ridge beyond the McPherson barn, the Battle of Gettysburg began about 8:00 AM with Heth's Confederate division attacking the dismounted cavalry of General John Buford's division. As infantry reinforcements arrived on both sides, the fighting spread along this ridge from the Hagerstown Road to Oak Hill. To your right is the Lutheran Seminary whose cupola was used as an observation post by both sides during the 3-day battle. Also to your right along the Chambersburg Pike (Route 30) is the location of General Robert E. Lee's headquarters on July 2 and 3, 1863.

 This monument marks the spot where General John Reynolds fell after being struck by a stray bullet on the morning of July 1.

② The equestrian statue of General Reynolds and that of General Buford mark the spot where Calef's battery first engaged Heth's Confederates. One of the cannon barrels at the base of Buford's statue was the actual cannon that opened the battle.

③ **Railway Cut**   One regiment of Davis' Confederate Brigade sought cover in this cut only to be trapped when Union troops appeared on the crests. Over 200 Confederates and the colors of the regiment were captured.

2 **Peace Light Memorial**   This impressive monument is located on strategic Oak Hill where Rodes' Confederate division attacked the flanks of the Union I and XI corps during the early afternoon of July 1. The memorial was dedicated in 1938 by President Roosevelt in a 75th anniversary service attended by more than 1800 Civil War veterans. The flame is fed by natural gas.

3 **Oak Ridge**   At this location, Rodes launched an ill-fated attack with two brigades against the right flank of the I corps line. It was repulsed by Robinson's division with heavy Confederate losses. The observation platform affords an excellent view of the XI corps line in the valley below.

④ **Lee's Retreat**   On July 4th, General Lee and the Army of Northern Virginia began its retreat to Hagerstown down what is now Route 116.

4 **North Carolina Monument** An impressive statue located where A.P. Hill's Corps formed for the assault on July 3. It was sculptured by Gutzon Borglum of Mount Rushmore fame. It was dedicated in 1929.

5 Tennessee State Memorial, last of the Confederate State memorials, dedicated in 1983.

6 **Confederate Artillery** For the last mile, the road has followed the Confederate artillery positions used during the great cannonade preceding the assault on July 3. Refer to the Artillery section in this book for data and pictures of the various types of cannon.

5 **Virginia Memorial** Dedicated in 1917 by the state of Virginia, it includes an excellent statue of General Robert E. Lee on his horse Traveller. It should be noted here that General Lee is the only Confederate officer with a statue.

7 Florida State Memorial

8 Mississippi State Memorial
Louisiana State Memorial

6 **Pitzer Woods** On the afternoon of July 2, McLaws' Division of Longstreet's Corps formed along this ridge and woods line before launching their attack against Sickles' III Corps salient around the Peach Orchard.

9 **Warfield Ridge Tower** From this tower, an excellent view of the Peach Orchard is seen to the east. To the west is former President Eisenhower's farm.

10 Georgia State Memorial
South Carolina State Memorial
Arkansas State Memorial

(11) Texas State Memorial
Alabama State Memorial
Confederate States Memorial

7 **Warfield Ridge**   This position marked the extreme right of Hood's division, Longstreet's Corps, prior to their attack against the Union III Corps and Little Round Top. Longstreet's two divisions eventually shattered Sickles' advanced line and drove them from the field.

(12)
BIG ROUND TOP
Loop Trail

TO BEGIN YOUR WALK
From the parking area roadside steps, an asphalt pathway leads one-quarter mile to the 585 foot summit of Big Round Top. The hill rises two hundred feet above the parking area. The Loop Trail begins on the left of the asphalt pathway, about 90 feet from the steps. This dirt, loop trail leads clockwise around Big Round Top. The trail has gradual inclines and is about one mile in length. Numbered posts along the way correspond to the stops indicated in this folder.

8 **Little Round Top**   This hill was a key position in the Union line but was left undefended when Sickles advanced his corps on the afternoon of July 2. The Confederate attempt to take it was thwarted by General Gouverneur Warren who summoned Colonel Strong Vincent's Brigade in the nick of time. In the bloody fight, Colonel Vincent was killed as was General Weed whose brigade came to Vincent's aid. Lieutenant Hazlett, the battery commander who struggled to get his guns to the summit was also killed.

9 **The Wheatfield**   During the afternoon of July 2 this field of wheat changed hands several times. Both sides kept sending in fresh units and by nightfall over 6,000 dead and wounded covered the trampled wheat. It remained in Confederate hands until the evening of July 3 when McCandless' Brigade retook the field without opposition.

⑬ The Loop   On this rise, Tilton's and Sweitzer's Union Brigades were pushed back by Confederate General Kershaw's assault and exposed the flank of the Wheatfield and Peach Orchard line.

❿ Peach Orchard   This Orchard was the center of Sickle's line. Much larger in 1863 than today, it bristled with cannon on the afternoon of July 2. Heavily assaulted by Wofford's and Barksdale's Confederate Brigades, the Union line here collapsed in a rout.

⑭ Trostle Farm   Union General Daniel Sickles established his III Corps headquarters here on the afternoon of July 2. Following the collapse of the Peach Orchard salient, Sickles was near the barn directing troops when his leg was hit by an artillery shell. The shattered limb was amputated that night.

⑮ Bigelow's Battery   During the retreat of the III Corps, the Ninth Massachusetts Battery under Captain Bigelow made a heroic stand at the Trostle barn. Without infantry support, this lone battery delayed several Confederate assaults by Barksdale's Brigade before four of his six guns were captured.

⓫ Plum Run Line   Following the retreat of the III Corps on the evening of July 2, about 15 cannons scraped together by Colonel McGilvery from various artillery batteries formed along this rise and closed a dangerous gap in the Union line until infantry reinforcements arrived.

⑯ New York Officers Memorial   Erected by the State of New York in recognition of service rendered by brigade commanders and above from the state of New York.

⑰ Minnesota Monument   This memorial stands near the spot where the 1st Minnesota Regiment launched their heroic counterattack against Willcox's Confederate Brigade. The regiment suffered over 82% casualties for their gallant effort in saving the line on July 2.

⓬ Pennsylvania Memorial   This outstanding monument erected by the Commonwealth of Pennsylvania honors the 34,530 Pennsylvanians who fought at Gettysburg. Their names are listed in bronze along the base, while statues and names of officers are listed along the top.

⑬ Spangler's Spring   This spring and the nearby earthworks were captured on the night of July 2 by Johnson's Confederate division only to be lost the next morning to Union XII Corps troops. Earthworks and fences constructed by Union troops can still be seen to the north of the spring.

⑱ Indiana State Memorial

⑲ This road generally follows the line of Union earthworks. Many reconstructed trenches can still be seen.

⑳ **Culp's Hill**   Defended stubbornly by General George Greene's Brigade on the night of July 2, the Confederates of Johnson's Division failed to capture this vital position. The tower on the summit gives an excellent view of Cemetery Hill.

㉑ **Steven's Knoll**   The artillery on this knoll delivered a deadly fire into Hay's and Avery's Brigades during their attack against East Cemetery Hill on the evening of July 2. The statue is of General Henry Slocum, commander of the Union XII Corps at Gettysburg.

⑭ East Cemetery Hill   After their rout on July 1, Union troops rallied on this hill. On July 2, the Confederates of Hay's and Avery's Brigades briefly captured the batteries on the summit but were repulsed after dark. Across the Baltimore Pike is the Civil War period Cemetery Gatehouse.

㉒ **Hancock Statue**   Equestrian statue of Major General Winfield Hancock, commander of the Union II Corps at Gettysburg.

㉓ **Howard Statue**   Equestrian statue of Major General Oliver Howard, commander of the Union XI Corps at Gettysburg.

㉔ **Vermont Memorial**   Stannard's Vermont Brigade launched their counterattack from this point against Pickett's right flank and were instrumental in the failure of the Confederate attack on the afternoon of July 3.

㉕ **U.S. Regulars Monument**   Erected by the Congress to honor the Infantry, Cavalry, and Artillery units of the regular army who fought with the Union Army at Gettysburg.

15 **High Water Mark**   In this clump of trees and along the nearby stone fences, the spearhead of "Pickett's Charge" pierced the Union line on July 3. The Confederate forces had advanced for over a mile to this point before being repulsed by Union counter-attacks.

This walk begins on the back patio of the Cyclorama Center

26

HIGH WATER MARK
Walking Tour

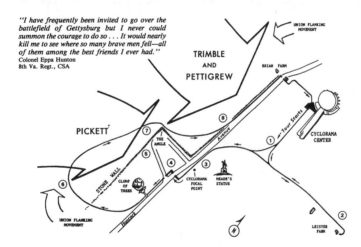

"I have frequently been invited to go over the battlefield of Gettysburg but I never could summon the courage to do so . . . It would nearly kill me to see where so many brave men fell—all of them among the best friends I ever had."
Colonel Eppa Hunton
8th Va. Regt., CSA

The Leister house, General Meade's headquarters on July 2-3, 1863.

13

16 **National Monument and Cemetery**
The National Cemetery was dedicated November 19, 1863 in a ceremony made famous by Lincoln's Gettysburg Address. Here lie buried, known and unknown, the Union dead that fell at Gettysburg. The impressive National Soldier's Monument stands near the spot where Lincoln delivered his address.

27

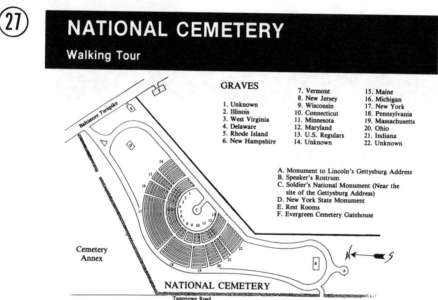

NATIONAL CEMETERY
Walking Tour

GRAVES

1. Unknown
2. Illinois
3. West Virginia
4. Delaware
5. Rhode Island
6. New Hampshire
7. Vermont
8. New Jersey
9. Wisconsin
10. Connecticut
11. Minnesota
12. Maryland
13. U.S. Regulars
14. Unknown
15. Maine
16. Michigan
17. New York
18. Pennsylvania
19. Massachusetts
20. Ohio
21. Indiana
22. Unknown

A. Monument to Lincoln's Gettysburg Address
B. Speaker's Rostrum
C. Soldier's National Monument (Near the site of the Gettysburg Address)
D. New York State Monument
E. Rest Rooms
F. Evergreen Cemetery Gatehouse

Cemetery Annex

NATIONAL CEMETERY

Taneytown Road

The following list of memorials or points of interest are not included in the guide because they are not along the tour route or they have been recently added. Refer to the map on the back cover for their location.

1 John Burns Statue

2 Gettysburg College was called Pennsylvania College in 1863. The main hall was used as a hospital during and following the battle.

3 Wheelers and Dilgers Batteries—These two XI Corps batteries were instrumental in the repulse of Rodes' attack against the I Corps on Oak Ridge.

4 Barlow Knoll—This small knoll marked the extreme right of the XI Corps line on July 1. The arrival of General Jubal Early's Confederate Division returning from York attacked and overran this position and caused the entire Union line to collapse.

5 President Dwight David Eisenhower retired to his farm at Gettysburg following his eight years in the White House. He used an office on the campus of Gettysburg College which later became the Eisenhower House. The statue was dedicated in 1970 by the college in memory of its distinguished neighbor.

In the fields around the Culp farm, the Eisenhower farm is located west of the Warfield Ridge tower and is open to the public via a shuttle bus.

6 In the fields around the Culp farm, General Early formed the brigades of Hays and Avery for their attack on Cemetery Hill during the evening hours of July 2.

7 Confederate troops of General Edward Johnson's Division advanced through this area to attack Union positions on Culp's Hill and Spangler's Spring.

8 **Devils Den** Portions of Confederate General Hood's Division fought bitterly for this maze of boulders, finally dislodging the Union troops of Ward's Brigade. The Confederates used the excellent cover for sharpshooters which made life unpleasant for the Union troops on Little Round Top.

9 **Smith's New York Battery** These four 10-pound Parrotts covered the extreme left of the III Corps line on July 2. After several determined attacks, the Confederates succeeded in capturing three of the four guns at this location.

10 Statue of Major General John Sedgewick, commander of the Union VI Corps at Gettysburg. It is interesting to note here that the equestrian statues on the field are coded although it was not intentional. If the horse has one hoof off the ground, the officer was wounded. If the horse has two hoofs in the air, the officer was killed. General Sedgewick was neither as is noted by the horse, however, he was to lose his life to a sharpshooter's bullet at the Battle of Spotsylvania a year later.

East Cavalry Battlefield Located 3 miles east of Gettysburg on the Hanover Road (Route 116), See Cavalry Battle Section on page 64.

The granite boulders of Devils Den, scene of heavy fighting on July 2, 1863.

15

THE ARMIES

ARMY OF THE POTOMAC United States of America

Composed of 19 Divisions in 7 Corps—51 Brigades total—95,000 infantry

Major General George G. Meade, Commanding
Major General Daniel Butterfield, Chief of Staff
Major General Gouverneur Warren, Chief Engineer
Major General Alfred Pleasonton, Chief of Cavalry
Brigadier General Henry Hunt, Chief of Artillery

The Army of the Potomac was composed of infantry regiments from the following states:

Pennsylvania—69	Maine—9	New Hampshire—3
New York—62	Michigan—7	Delaware—1
Massachusetts—18	Wisconsin—6	Rhode Island—1
New Jersey—12	Connecticut—5	Illinois—1
Ohio—12	Indiana—5	West Virginia—1
Regular Army Units—10	Indiana—5	Minnesota—1
Vermont—10	Maryland—3	

The Army of the Potomac used badges to identify its Corps as follows:

I Corps ●	V Corps ✠	XI Corps ☽
II Corps ♣	VI Corps ✚	XII Corps ★
III Corps ◆		

The Divisions within a Corps were identified by the color of the Corps emblem; red for first division, white for second division, blue for third division. The appropriate corps emblem appears on all regimental and brigade markers.

ARMY OF NORTHERN VIRGINIA Confederate States of America

Composed of 9 Divisions in 3 Corps—37 Brigades total—73,000 infantry

General Robert E. Lee, Commanding
Major General James E.B. Stuart, Chief of Cavalry
Brigadier General William Pendleton, Chief of Artillery

The Army of Northern Virginia was composed from the infantry regiments from the following states:

Virginia—41	South Carolina—11	Florida—3
Georgia—34	Mississippi—11	Texas—3
North Carolina—31	Louisiana—10	Arkansas—1
Alabama—16	Tennessee—4	Maryland—1

The Army of Northern Virginia did not use emblems to identify its Corps.

GETTYSBURG ADDRESS
November 19, 1863

Fourscore and seven years ago, our fathers brought forth on this continent a new nation, conceived in liberty, and dedicated to the proposition that all men are created equal. Now we are engaged in a great civil war, testing whether that nation, or any nation so conceived and so dedicated, can long endure. We are met on a great battlefield of that war. We have come to dedicate a portion of that field as a final resting-place for those who here gave their lives that that nation might live. It is altogether fitting and proper that we should do this. But in a larger sense we cannot dedicate, we cannot consecrate, we cannot hallow this ground. The brave men, living and dead, who struggled here, have consecrated it far above our poor power to add or detract. The world will little note, nor long remember, what we say here, but it can never forget what they did here. It is for us, the living, rather to be dedicated here to the unfinished work which they who fought here have thus far so nobly advanced. It is rather for us to be here dedicated to the great task remaining before us, — that from these honored dead we take increased devotion to that cause for which they gave the last full measure of devotion, — that we here highly resolve that these dead shall not have died in vain, — that this nation, under God, shall have a new birth of freedom, — and that government of the people, by the people, for the people, shall not perish from the earth.

Abraham Lincoln

17

An artillery battery in action

Caisson and limber

ARTILLERY

Civil War cannon had advanced little since the early days of artillery. Guns and ammunition were unreliable as well as dangerous to operate.

Barrels or tubes were made from iron or bronze and gun carriages were built of white oak with iron fittings. Many types came into use during the war, ranging from small howitzers to huge seige guns. At Gettysburg however, only field cannon and howitzers were in use due to the mobility required in the campaign.

When unlimbered, horses and caissons were moved to the rear or a safe place nearby. The gun was aligned by hand, loaded and fired. Upon firing, the gun would recoil a few feet or up to a dozen yards, depending on the powder charge and amount of ammunition.

After firing, it was rolled back by hand and re-aligned, being swabbed and loaded as it went. An efficient crew could load, aim and fire twice in one minute. When under heavy attack, crews had been known to fire four canister shots in a minute. Swabbing the barrel could not be hurried for not only did it help cool the tube, but it also extinguished any lingering sparks before the next charge was inserted.

Attacking infantry usually made batteries their prime targets, for the capture of field pieces were a great prize. Often as crews were limbering up to pull out, assaulting infantry would shoot the horses, requiring the piece to be abandoned. If capture was unavoidable, crews would even shoot their own horses to prevent the enemy from moving the piece. Spiking the weapon, that is to drive a piece of metal into the firing vent, also rendered it inoperative for a time.

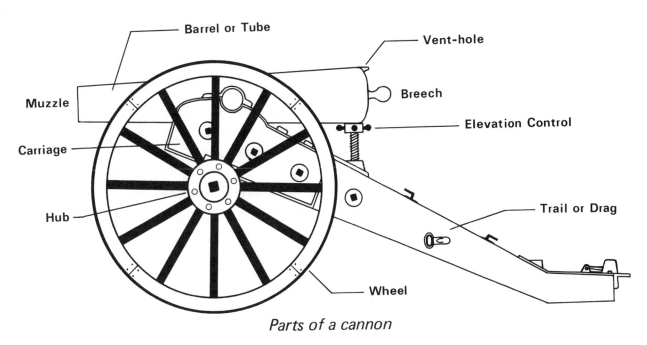

Parts of a cannon

AMMUNITION

Ammunition among field artillery in the Civil War fell into four types; solid, shell, case (shrapnel), and canister. Chests of artillery pieces carried all types in amounts depending on the type of action anticipated. Generally speaking the types are as follows:

Solid Solid shot was a solid iron shell, primarily used on cavalry, infantry in column or infantry taken in flank. It was used in a bowling ball effect and was the most accurate of the four types. Artillery nomenclatured as pounders (i.e. Ten-Pounder) get it from the weight of one round of its solid shot.

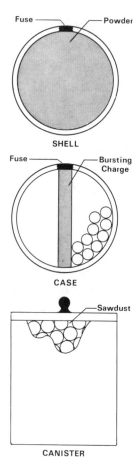

Shell Explosive shell was a hollow projectile filled with about 90% black powder. Fuses were cut to time (0 – 5 sec.) and lit by the firing charge. Shell was used primarily against fortifications and enemy artillery.

Case (Shrapnel) Case shot was invented by General Shrapnel of the British Army, and comprised a hollow shell filled with about 75 iron balls and a bursting charge. It was used against infantry at long range (over 400 yards) and most effective when set to explode about 15 feet overhead.

Canister Canister was a thin metal can containing iron or lead balls in sawdust. In a Napoleon, 25-27 one inch balls were used. When fired, the can ruptured on leaving the muzzle and the effect was like a huge shotgun. Canister was used only in defense against attacking infantry.

Ammunition in the Civil War was notoriously unreliable. Duds were common, sometimes as high as 50% failures. Powder used was the old black type, producing immense clouds of sulfur smoke, blotting out targets and irritating gunners and supporting infantry alike.

Union Union forces fired over 33,000 rounds during the three days of Gettysburg. This expended about 34% of their supply. Seven pieces were lost to the enemy and artillerymen suffered 769 killed, wounded, or missing. Several hundred horses were also killed or had to be destroyed.

Confederate Confederate forces fired about 22,000 rounds but this expended over 50% of their supply. Six pieces were lost and they suffered 608 casualties in the three days fighting.

12-POUNDER (NAPOLEON) Perhaps the most commonly used cannon, the Napoleons dot the battlefield marking the batteries of both sides. Distinguished by their green barrels, twelve-pounders comprised 40% of the cannon used at Gettysburg.

Developed for the Army of Napoleon III, twelve-pounders were muzzle-loading, bronze barreled (90% copper, 10% tin), field artillery. Their immense weight, 2,600 pounds, made mobility difficult for the six horses required to pull it and its full caissons. A crew of six men usually manned each piece.

Capable of four canister shots per minute, Napoleons proved to be efficient killers of infantry. Firing canister at massed troops under 400 yards distance had a devastating effect as Union artillery proved on July 3 against Pickett's assault.

Napoleons had a low muzzle velocity due to its smooth bore design. Its range was short, under one mile (1700 yards) for solid shot and less for shell (1300 yards). The caisson chests carried 32 rounds of the four types of ammunition. Powder charge used for solid and shell was usually 2½ pounds of black powder.

An excellent example of a Napoleon in mint condition stands in the museum area of the Cyclorama Center.

WHITWORTH RIFLE The forerunner of modern artillery, breech-loading Whitworths greatly increased the range of artillery. As a breech-loader, tighter rifling was possible as the shell did not need to be rammed the length of the barrel as in a muzzle-loader. The result was ranges up to five miles.

Brought through the blockade from England, these advanced guns were never available in sufficient numbers to the South. Union artillerymen had decided the breech-loader to be of little value and never employed them in great numbers. The North had none at Gettysburg.

The Whitworth fired an elongated twelve-pound shell with a peculiar whine that distinguished it from the lower velocity muzzle-loaders.

Two Whitworths on the field are located to the left of the Peace Light Memorial. They are easily recognized by their unusual breech mechanism.

PARROTT RIFLES The Parrotts were muzzle-loading rifles, distinguished by their cast barrels with a reinforcing band of wrought iron around the breech. Ten-pounders were the widest used, with a barrel weight of only 900 pounds and a range of 6,000 yards (3 miles).

Twenty-pounders were classed as light seige or heavy field artillery. Their weight made mobility difficult at no increase in range over a ten-pounder.

3-INCH ORDNANCE RIFLE Made by wrapping boiler plate around a core, 3-inch rifles were light weight and long ranged. With a barrel weight of only 820 pounds, it became the exclusive weapon of the fast moving Horse Artillery. As a favorite of many regular army batteries, it became known as the Ordnance.

The 3-inch Ordnance was a muzzle-loader with a range of about 4,000 yards (2 miles). Its ammunition chests carried a substantial 50 rounds.

ARTILLERY ORGANIZATION

Union   Chief of Artillery: Brig General Henry J. Hunt

Each infantry corps was assigned one artillery brigade; the cavalry corps assigned two artillery brigades, and five brigades went into the Artillery Reserve under the command of Brig General Robert Tyler. Generally, there were five or six batteries to an artillery brigade. The Union forces had 68 batteries present at Gettysburg for 362 cannons.

A Union battery usually consisted of six guns divided into three, 2-gun sections (left, middle and right section). The guns in a battery were of the same type making ammunition supplies easier to maintain. About 100 men were required to man a Union battery.

Confederate   Chief of Artillery: Brig General William Pendleton

Confederate artillery was also divided among the Corps with a smaller Artillery Reserve. The Southern forces also had 68 batteries present, but since a Confederate battery had just four guns, they unlimbered only 272 cannons.

Southern batteries were of mixed types of guns, making ammunition supply extremely difficult. A force of 65 men maintained a Confederate battery.

WHY INVASION?

By June of 1863, the *Army of Northern Virginia* had an impressive record. First Bull Run had shown the Federal Government that the Confederate States would not give in easily to their authority. The long, drawn out Peninsular Campaign, the series of battles through the Seven Days and the Union defeat at Second Bull Run finally drove the Union forces from the gates of Richmond.

The Battle of Antietam, a Union victory in the sense that they had succeeded in forcing *Lee* back to Virginia, was more a draw in that the vastly superior Union forces failed to destroy the *Army of Northern Virginia*. The later battles of Fredericksburg and Chancellorsville were no less than impressive victories for *Lee* and the South.

Now this army, that caused the dismissal of three Union Commanders and on its way to a fourth, that defeated every Union force sent into Virginia, was to undertake another invasion of the North.

In one sense, the first attempt at Antietam had indeed resulted in a defeat. The lack of a decisive victory did result in the loss of the immediate chance of recognition by Britian or France. The South would have to go it alone.

In spite of its victories, the *Army of Northern Virginia* was in a battered condition. What it had in spirit and determination was dimmed by deteriorated weapons, lack of food, clothing, shoes, and ammunition. The Army of the Potomac, though defeated many times, had only to fall back on the Washington defenses. Here it could refit and fill its ranks, then resume its pressure on the dwindling resources of the South.

Lee's decision to invade the North stemmed from these conditions. The two years of war and victories had served only to weaken the South and do no appreciable damage to the North. The obvious answer was to move northward, drawing the Union Army away from Washington and the Federal Fleet. There it could be destroyed, communications and supply lines wrecked, and the way opened for the capture of Washington and other northern cities.

The urgency of a decisive move was apparent. Although in the east the Confederates were holding their own, in the west their vitals were being torn away. *Lee* could not send any worthwhile forces west as his army was already inferior to anything the Union could muster. The west, though important, would have to go its own way. For *Lee* knew that the war could be lost in the west, but it would have to be won in the east. What good would the capture of Vicksburg or Chattanooga gain the Union if *Lee* could crush the Army of the Potomac on its home ground? A victory of this caliber would insure the success of the Confederate States.

The depleted resources of the South was another reason for an invasion. Food was perhaps the most vital priority and the Pennsylvania harvest time was

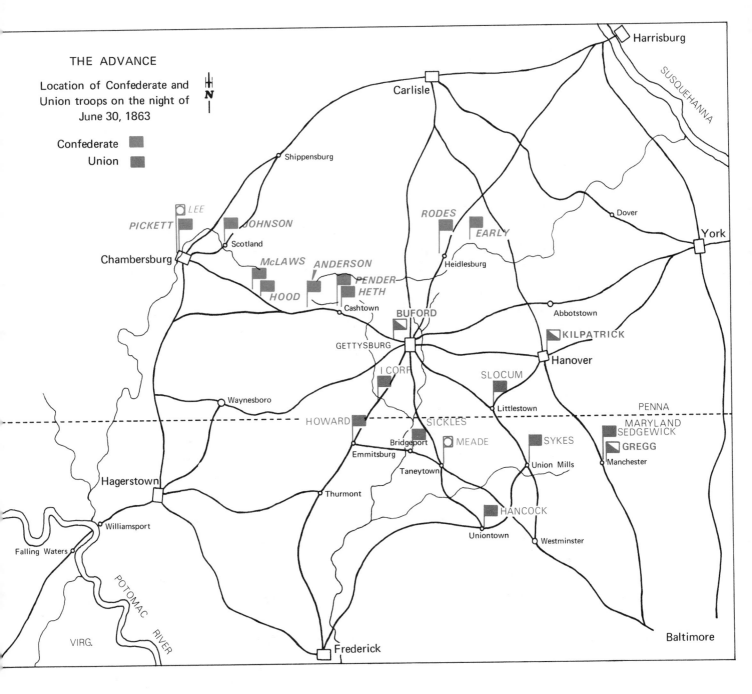

THE ADVANCE

Location of Confederate and
Union troops on the night of
June 30, 1863

Confederate
Union

drawing near. The rich farmland of the north could supply a Southern Army for a long time. Horses, clothing, shoes, almost everything needed by the deprived army laid beyond the Potomac.

General *Longstreet* had favored a strike through Tennessee and Kentucky and possibly into Ohio, forcing a Union withdrawl from around Vicksburg. But to *Lee* and eventually *President Davis*, Pennsylvania offered the greatest promise of a southern victory to gain independence. The decision was made, and on the third of June, 1863, the *Army of Northern Virginia* began to break camp. Westward, then northward, the dedicated, tough southerners headed for Pennsylvania and an undeserved defeat.

EVENTS LEADING TO GETTYSBURG

The true epic of Gettysburg, though spawned in Virginia, had its violent birth on McPhersons heights to the west of the town. This low ridge, running southward from Oak Hill along Willoubly Run, follows its sister ridge with the Seminary for nearly two miles. On these two ridges and the plateau connecting them, began the most important three days in the history of the United States.

To be sure, when James Gettys founded the town in 1780, he could not imagine that this town would become the most famous battlefield in the country. For that matter, *Lee* and Meade would not have picked this site if given a choice.

The chance meeting came as a result of General *Jubal Early's* Division passing through Gettysburg on the evening of June 26. *Early* had demanded clothing and provisions, along with $10,000 in currency. The town authorities had assured him the requests were impossible, and, needing to move on to York at daybreak, left the town relatively untouched. He did, however, send word back to *A.P. Hill's III* Corps, moving eastward from Chambersburg, that the town possessed a supply of shoes.

On the morning of June 30, General *Henry Heth's* Division was bivouacked near Cashtown, eight miles west of Gettysburg. Recalling General *Early's* message about the shoes, *Heth* directed General *James Pettigrew's* Brigade to move to Gettysburg and check out *Early's* report. *Pettigrew* mustered his brigade and marched off toward Gettysburg preceded by the usual skirmish line.

A series of delays caused *Pettigrew* to arrive on the high ground west of the town late in the day. Although the town rang with excitement at the approach of the Confederates, he observed that it was unoccupied by Union troops. He sent the skirmishers forward and ordered his brigade to prepare to move out.

Before the brigade could advance, scouts reported a large body of soldiers moving north on the Emmitsburg Road. It turned out to be a sizeable force of Union cavalry, consisting of two brigades of General John Buford's Division, acting as the advance force of the Union left wing. They rode into Gettysburg and began nudging *Pettigrew* back. The retirement was slow and grudging, but there was little exchange of fire. Both commanders were unwilling to initiate a major action and *Pettigrew* withdrew to his former position near Cashtown.

Pettigrew was most reluctant to give up the needed shoes. He rode to Division Headquarters at Cashtown to report the encounter. As he reported to *Heth*, *A.P. Hill*, the Corps commander arrived and also listened to *Pettigrew's* account. Both *Heth* and *Hill* discounted *Pettigrew's* assumption that it was regular army and not militia. When *Heth* asked to move his division to Gettysburg the next morning, *Hill* gave his permission.

During evening hours, Buford's Cavalry had established itself on Herr's and McPherson's Ridge and sent pickets out to the north and west. Buford, with only two of his brigades and one battery of artillery, settled down for the night. He was fully aware that the enemy would advance on his position in force in the morning.

Maj Gen John Buford, USA (LC)

Maj Gen Henry Heth, CSA (LC)

THE FIRST DAY
Wednesday July 1, 1863

At five o'clock in the morning, Major General *Henry Heth* put his division on the road to Gettysburg. Of his four brigades, Brigadier General *James Archer's* Alabama and Tennessee regiments led the column, followed by the brigades of *Davis, Brockenborough,* and *Pettigrew.* At the last minute, out of either fear or hope of a major action, *III* Corps commander *A.P. Hill* ordered General Dorsey *Pender's* Division to follow *Heth.*

Where the Cashtown Pike crosses Marsh Creek, *Archer's* skirmishers ran into the first Union troops. An advance patrol of Gamble's Brigade appeared from the woods and *Heth* quickly formed a battle line. *Archer's* Brigade deployed south of the Cashtown Pike, *Davis* to the north. *Pettigrew* and *Brockenborough* remained in column on the road. Once formed, the line began its advance once again. As the Confederate skirmish line approached the Marsh Creek bridge, Lieutenant Marcellus Jones of the 8th Illinois Cavalry fired the first shot of the battle.*

*Some claim troopers from the 9th New York cavalry fired the first shots.

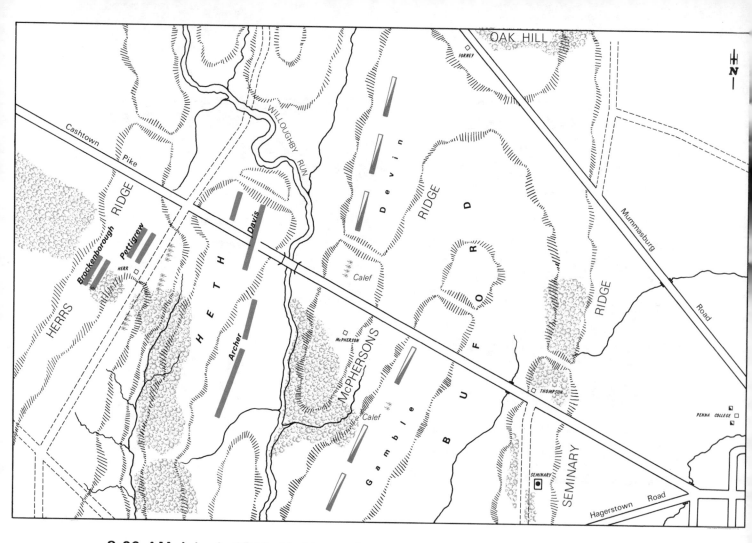

8:00 AM July 1, 1863, McPherson's Ridge   Buford's Union Cavalry Brigades are attacked by two brigades of *Heth's* Confederate Division.

THE OPENING PHASE

General Buford was now warned of the Confederate approach. He immediately sent word to General Reynolds that Southern infantry was moving in force toward Gettysburg. Through the light drizzle that was falling, the sound of firing could be heard to the west as *Heth* rolled back the Union pickets. The time was nearing seven o'clock.

Buford's Cavalry Division was normally mounted, but when dismounted, they were tough infantry fighters. Armed with breech-loading rifles, they could deliver a rate of fire equal to a much larger unit. Joined with Calef's battery of six 3-inch guns, they presented a fairly strong line along McPherson's Ridge.

Heth's Division arrived on Herr's Ridge as his skirmish line made contact with Buford's troopers. He thought at first infantry was occupying the heights, so before committing his units he waited for *Pender's* Division to arrive and support him. In the meantime, his skirmishers began probing for weak points in the Union line.

28

The Union Cavalry cleverly concealed their weakness and maintained an effective defense. Though numbering more than 2500 men, this was substantially reduced by the necessity of holding the horses, a major drawback of fighting dismounted. Nevertheless, by eight o'clock, General *Heth* became convinced he faced only a small cavalry unit and meant to sweep it aside and move into Gettysburg. He ordered *Archer* and *Davis*, still in battle formation, to attack.

Buford's troops immediately began to feel the pressure. The early morning drizzle stopped but the sulfur smoke of battle closed the sky in around them. Return fire became murderous and Confederate artillery began finding its range. By eight-thirty, Buford had committed his last reserves. The blue ranks began to thin and their returning fire dropped accordingly. Not only that, but the sheer number of Confederates began spilling over the flanks. Buford knew that time was rapidly running out and prepared to withdraw his troopers to Cemetery Hill.

At this stage of the battle, an officer of the Signal Corps in the cupola of the Lutheran Seminary spotted an infantry column on the Emmitsburg Road. General

10:00 AM July 1, 1863, McPherson's Ridge   Buford's Cavalry was relieved by Wadsworth's Division of the I Corps. Meredith's attack through McPherson's Woods surprised *Archer's* Brigade and captured over 1000 Confederates. To the north, *Davis'* Brigade overran Cutler's positions and forced his retreat to Seminary Ridge.

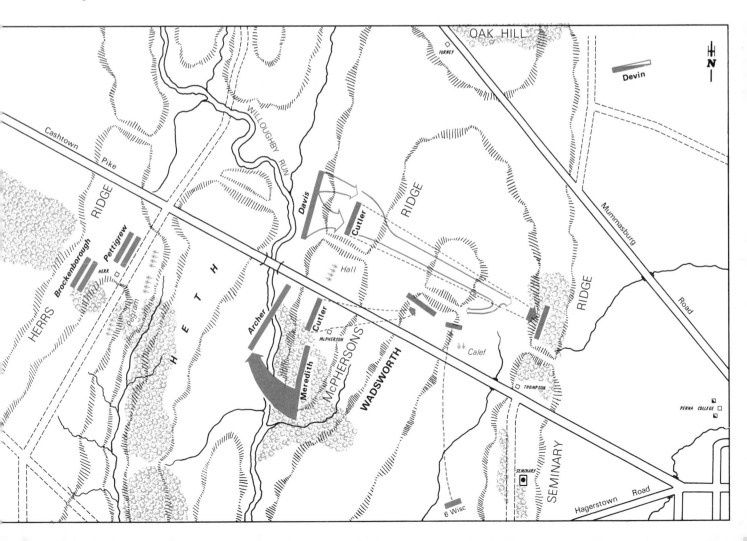

A regiment drawn up in battle formation with its skirmish line advanced

Buford was summoned and watched the column long enough to be certain it was Reynolds and the Union I Corps. With a glance to the northwest he wondered if they would arrive in time. For in the smoky distance, the Cashtown Pike was filled with *Pender's* marching columns.

Major General John Reynolds arrived on the field at approximately eight-thirty and was directed to the Seminary by Buford's aide. Here he met the cavalry commander and discussed the situation. After a quick study of the terrain, he decided to hold this position. Following this decision which would forever change Gettysburg, he rode back to direct the Corps onto the field. It was to be one of his last decisions for the Army of the Potomac, but it was also to be the most important. The Battle of Gettysburg was now on in earnest.

McPHERSON'S RIDGE

The vanguard of the Corps was General James Wadsworth's Division, with the brigades of Lysander Cutler and Solomon Meredith. As they reached Seminary Ridge, Reynolds himself took command and directed them into line, relieving Buford's troops. Reynolds ordered three regiments of Cutler's Brigade north of the railway cut and deployed Cutler's two remaining regiments and Meredith's famous Iron Brigade south of the Cashtown Pike, extending into McPherson's woods. *Heth* became suddenly aware he was no longer facing dismounted cavalry. With their bands playing and colors uncased, the Army of the Potomac made known its arrival on the field.

30

Archer's and Davis' Brigades, supported by heavy artillery fire, were crossing Willoubly Run as Reynolds was deploying his infantry. The lines facing each other were off balance, that is, Meredith's line overlapped Archer; Davis' overlapped Cutler. As a result, both Archer and Cutler were in danger of being flanked.

General Meredith no sooner had his brigade deployed than he began to attack. The left of his line, moving through McPherson's woods, suddenly burst out on Archer's flank and rear. In the wild melee that followed, nearly a thousand Confederate prisoners were taken, including General James Archer himself. The Iron Brigade drove Archer's troops back across Willoubly Run at bayonet point and planted themselves on the slopes of Herr's Ridge.

At the same time, Cutler was having a less than successful engagement. Davis outflanked his three regiments north of the railway cut and forced them back to Seminary Ridge. This opened a huge gap to the Union rear and left Hall's Artillery Battery entirely without support. Only by quick use of a reserve unit and Cutler's remaining regiments were they able to check Davis' advance and drive him back across Willoubly Run.

During the deployment of the Iron Brigade, General Reynolds had been carelessly exposing himself to fire from the Confederate snipers along Willoubly Run. While on the edge of McPherson's woods, as he was directing Meredith's Brigade into position, Major General John Reynolds was struck in the head by a minie' ball. He was killed instantly, slumping from his horse before his horrified aides. General Reynolds, only 43 years old, died an untimely death that was mourned by many on both sides. As a brillant soldier, his talents would be missed by Meade as sorely as Stonewall Jackson's were already missed by General Lee. His body was hastily removed from the field to avoid demoralizing the ranks of Union infantry he led.

Upon the death of Reynolds, command passed to acting Corps commander Major General Abner Doubleday. Although he would do a superb job this day, Doubleday would receive little credit for it. He would be blamed, unjustly, for the eventual collapse of the I Corps.

General Doubleday, after handling Cutler's counterattack, ordered the Iron Brigade back from Herr's Ridge. He again set the line as Reynolds had ordered. It was now a little after eleven o'clock. For General Heth it had been a miserable morning. His brigades of Archer's and Davis' had been badly hurt, losing half their effective force. He would now have to commit his reserve brigades, Pettigrew and Brockenborough, to carry the ridge.

Spencer's carbine

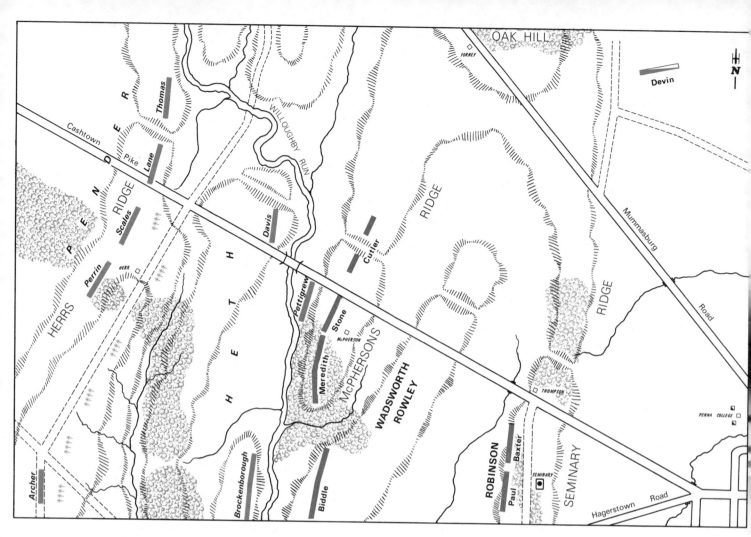

12:00 Noon July 1, 1863, McPherson's Ridge *Heth's* two fresh brigades launched an attack against the recently reinforced Union line. Repulsed, the Confederates began a cannonade of 80 guns against the Union troops.

THE UNION LINE STRENGTHENED

At about eleven-thirty, Doubleday at last received word that the remaining I Corps Divisions of Rowley's (Doubleday's) and Robinson's had arrived. This reinforcement was just in time, for *Heth's* fresh brigades were moving against the Union line. Doubleday quickly divided Rowley's two brigades on Meredith's flanks; Stone's on the right by the Cashtown Pike, Biddle's on the left extending the line to the Hagerstown Road. Robinson's two brigades were placed in reserve near the Luthern Seminary.

As Biddle was moving into position, *Brockenborough* struck his flank and front, threatening to turn the Union left. *Pettigrew*, picking up remnants of *Davis'* Brigade as he advanced, struck Stone's Brigade along the Pike. Although exposed and outnumbered, the Pennsylvanians in this brigade refused to yield their states soil to enemy infantry. Stone's bucktails stubbornly held their ground. After nearly an hour, *Heth* finally conceded his infantry could not carry the Union line. He ordered his men to break contact and fall back.

Confederate *III* Corps commander *A.P. Hill* had now arrived with *Pender's* Division and the entire Corps artillery, numbering some eighty guns. *Hill* could easily have swept McPherson's Ridge had he known General *Lee's* intentions and the true Union strength. Instead, he brought his mass of artillery to bear on the Union lines.

The Confederate cannonade commenced about twelve-thirty, inflicting more losses on the already battered I Corps. They had been fighting for nearly four hours when an observer in the Seminary cupola signaled to Doubleday that the Union XI Corps was approaching. The word was passed and cheers for Howard's Germans rolled along the line. Fifteen minutes later, Schurz's Division marched into Gettysburg.

OAK HILL

Upon his arrival on the field, Major General Oliver Howard took command of both Corps. He turned command of XI Corps over to General Schurz, then ordered his division(Schurz) and Barlows to link up with the I Corps and extend the line to Oak Hill. He also ordered Von Steinwehr's Division to position itself on Cemetery Hill and act as reserve.

The numerical advantage of the XI Corps was cancelled by the arrival of Major General *Robert Rodes'* Division, Confederate *II* Corps, advancing on the Newville Road. This division, five brigades strong, arrived as the XI Corps was moving out into the open fields north of the town. Lieutenant General *Richard Ewell*, the Corps commander riding with *Rodes*, saw the strategic advantage of Oak Hill and ordered *Rodes* to occupy it.

This quick move by *Rodes* not only denied the XI Corps its intended position, but also placed his division square on the right flank of the I Corps. *Rodes* was in a great position to inflict havoc on both Union Corps but for the time being that was not to be the case.

General Howard at once tried to rectify his orders. With Oak Hill taken, his line would have to face north. He ordered Schurz's Division, now under General Schimmelfennig, to place its left flank on the Mummasburg Road and for Barlow's Division to pick up the line and extend it to the Almshouse. This move, for whatever reason it was made, left a quarter mile gap between the two Corps.

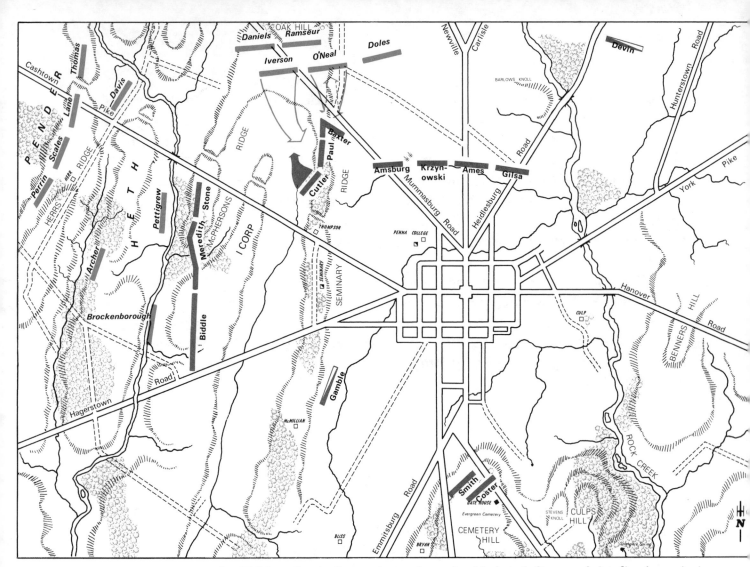

2:30 PM July 1, 1863 *Rodes'* attack against the Union I Corps right flank ended in failure when *O'Neal* and *Iverson* were repulsed with heavy losses.

FORNEY'S FIELD

General Doubleday saw at once the danger *Rodes'* Division presented to his I Corps. He quickly ordered Baxter's Brigade to extend the right flank to the Mummasburg Road. *Rodes* saw this brigade advancing and threw three regiments of *O'Neal's* Brigade against them. But Baxter's regiments, assisted by Wheeler's and Dilger's batteries in the valley below, threw *O'Neal's* badly led brigade back in disorder.

Iverson's Brigade was to advance with *O'Neal* and attack the flank of Baxter. In the confusion, they were late in getting started. The North Carolinians of *Iverson's* Brigade started crossing Forney's Field toward Baxter's flank just after *O'Neal* was repulsed. Baxter then was able to concentrate all his force against *Iverson*. Paul's Brigade, sent by Doubleday to support Baxter, moved up

The six "Napoleons" of Wheeler's Battery assisted Baxter's Brigade to repulse O'Neal's Confederates on Oak Ridge.

unnoticed and took position covering Baxter's flank. Hidden by a low stone wall, the Union line suddenly rose up and ripped *Iverson's* troops to shreds. Pinned down by Baxter and Paul, counterattacked on their right by Cutler, the brigade suffered over 800 casualties. Three of the four regiments were almost anniliated before they escaped beyond the Mummasburg Road.

Daniel's Brigade, intending to cover *Iverson's* right, became too confused and scattered to assist. Two regiments of its right ended up attacking Stone's Brigade on the Cashtown Pike. *Ramseur's* Brigade remained idle during this time on Oak Hill.

The attack of *Rodes'* Division had been a miserable failure. Badly led, badly supported, and no co-operation between the brigades caused heavy casualties on the division. Even *Dole's* Brigade, on the left of the division, was facing the XI Corps alone.

It was now nearly three o'clock. *Rodes* had been unsuccessful in his attack and *Heth*, in an effort to assist *Rodes*, again assaulted the Union line in McPherson's woods. *Brockenborough's* Brigade furiously attacked that position but was repulsed with losses by the tough Iron Brigade.

Iverson's Confederate Brigade suffered over 800 casualties while pinned down here in Forney's Field on the afternoon of July 1.

FLANKED AND ROUTED

But the tide now was beginning to turn, as it was bound to. The numerical superiority of the Confederates in men and artillery was starting to tell. General *A.P. Hill* was now determined to support *Heth's* Division and ordered three brigades of *Pender's* Division to move into the line. *Daniel's* Brigade, on Stone's right, was supported by regiments from *O'Neal* and *Ramseur*. For the I Corps, time was running out.

But the XI Corps in the valley was at that moment sealing everyones fate. Under heavy fire from *Rodes'* artillery on Oak Hill, the Corps advanced northward under threat from a new Confederate force on their right flank. Barlow directed the right of his line onto a knoll overlooking Rock Creek to meet this attack, and to flank *Dole's* Brigade to his left front. In executing this maneuver, Barlow exposed his right flank and rear to superior enemy forces. Without question, the XI Corps and eventually the I Corps were doomed unless Howard could reinforce the line.

Jubal Early's Division, returning from York and an unsuccessful attempt to cross the Susquehanna, had spent the night at Heidlesburg with *Rodes*. Their advance took different roads, delaying *Early*, but made his arrival a masterpiece of timing. It was going to spell disaster to both Union Corps.

General *John Gordon's* Georgia Brigade, forming the right of *Early's* battle line, waded Rock Creek and charged into the troops of Ames' Brigade on ''Barlow's Knoll''. Ames executed an orderly withdrawl back to his reserves in the Almshouse line. But no sooner than they took this position, they were struck on the flank by the brigades of *Hays* and *Avery*. Coster's Brigade rushed down from Cemetery Hill and Devin's Cavalry Brigade joined it in an attempt to stop the collapse. But the line was flanked and broken, throwing the XI Corps into a complete rout.

The I Corps, whose stand was nothing short of heroic, was now compelled to fight for its very life. The collapse of the XI Corps forced Baxter and Paul to withdraw under heavy fire to positions around the Seminary Ridge railcut. *Pender's* fresh division was now on the front line and stormed the slopes of McPherson's Ridge. Meredith's Brigade again repulsed its attackers, but the exposed regiments of Biddle's Brigade was forced to retreat, exposing the Iron Brigade's left flank. Stone and Meredith, after several more minutes of severe fighting, were compelled to fall back to Seminary Ridge. In desperation, Gamble's Brigade of exhausted cavalrymen were thrown in to stop *Lane's* Brigade moving on the Union left.

Fired by their success, *Pender's* Division, joined by *Daniels*, *Ramseur* and *O'Neal*, assaulted the Seminary Ridge line. Remnants of the I Corps, now mere shadows of their former strength, inflicted frightening losses on the Confederates.

For ten minutes or more the battle raged at point-blank range. Men fought with cannon swabs and bayonets, fence rails and rocks. Losses on both sides were enormous. But without support and against overwhelming odds, the Union troops were forced to retreat to Cemetery Hill.

Regiments and batteries fell back in disorder through the town. The streets were already jammed with Union troops from the XI Corps and now with the I Corps it became pure chaos. Fortunatly for the Union, the Confederates did not pursue in force and many units were able to make it to Cemetery Hill. Here they either rallied around Von Steinwehr's Division or continued to flee southward or eastward. Those that did stay were precious few.

SUMMARY—FIRST DAY

Union casualties were extremely high, with a total loss exceeding 9,000 men. Of this number, nearly 5,000 had been captured, mostly from the XI Corps in its rout. Out of 16,500 men deployed by the Union this left slightly more than 5500 troops to defend Cemetery Hill and its approaches.

The Confederate forces, though champions of the field, fared only a little better. Of the 22,000 men they put on the field only 5000 were in any condition for an attack. This was the time, many historians venture to say, the Confederates lost their golden chance. True, the occupation of Culp's Hill would have forced Meade to choose another position, but this would hardly have destroyed the Army of the Potomac. Even if an attack on Cemetery Hill would have been successful and it seems unlikely it would have, the destruction of the I and XI Corps would not have severly crippled Meade. The moral victory perhaps may have drawn recognition from Britian or France.

In actual units, the I and XI Corps put ten infantry and two cavalry brigades on the field, supported by ten artillery batteries. Confederate forces put fourteen brigades of infantry, supported by twenty batteries. The numerical superiority, though warranting victory, did not warrant such a complete rout as developed.

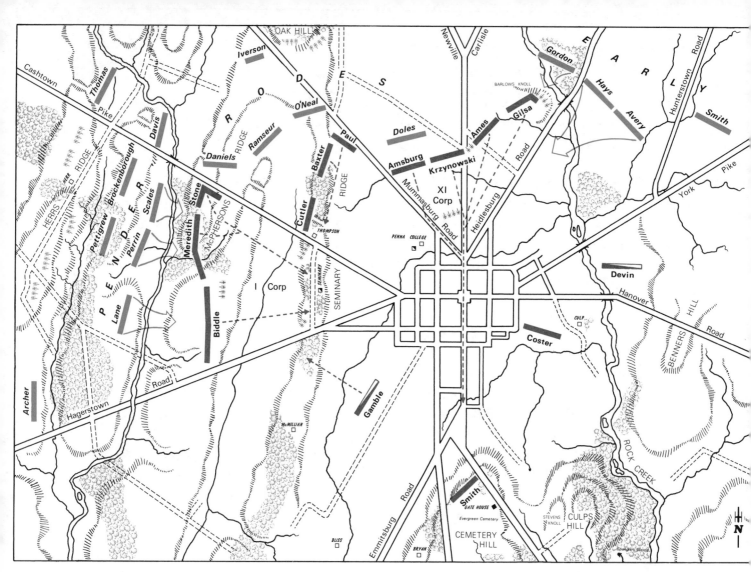

4:00 PM July 1, 1863 , The retreat of the Union troops through the town. When General *Early's* Division outflanked the XI Corps, the entire Union line collapsed.

General *Lee* arrived on the field about four-thirty and viewed the countryside from the Seminary cupola. Hundreds of dead and wounded covered the fields and roads in a bloody trail leading to Cemetery Hill. With plenty of daylight left, *Lee* surely would have wanted to attack, but by not knowing the whereabouts of the remaining Union Corps, he could not risk an attack against a force of unknown size. With *Stuart's* Cavalry absent, *Lee* had no recon forces with which to report location of Union forces.

By nightfall, because of lack of action on the part of Confederate commanders, namely *Ewell* and *Early*, no follow up assault was launched on Cemetery or Culps Hill. General *Ewell*, commanding *Jackson's* old Corps, wasted an excellent chance to crack the Union line again.

Locked now in conflict, both sides began calling in their far flung forces. Gettysburg, it would seem, would be a battlefield for yet another day.

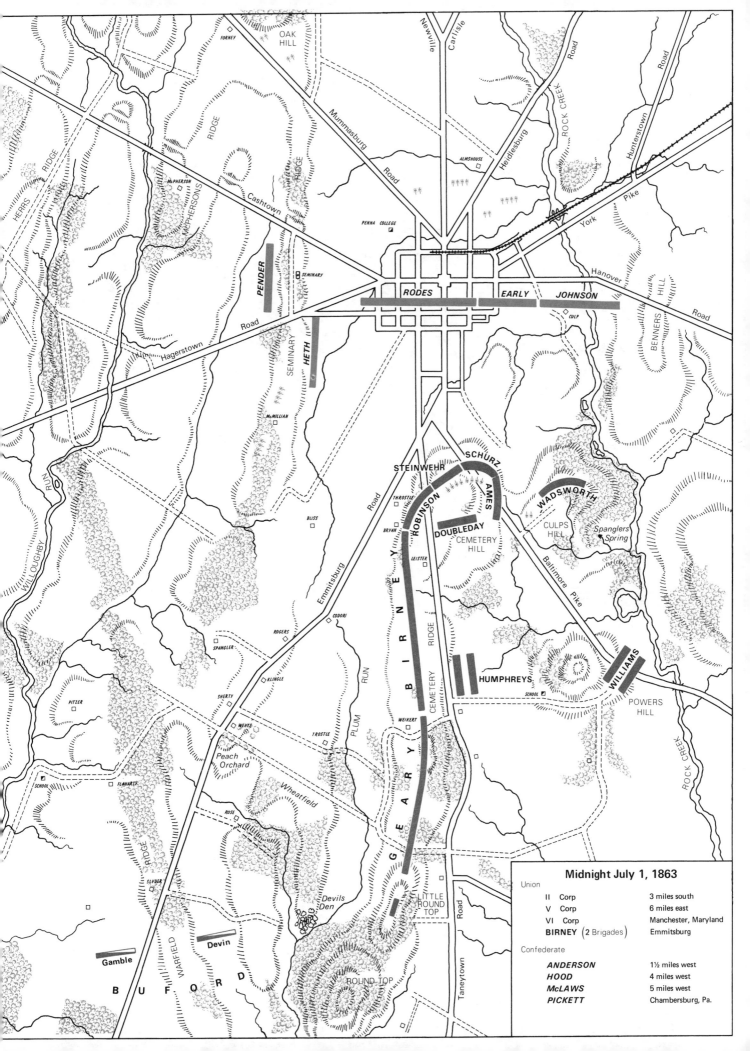

Midnight July 1, 1863

Union

II Corp — 3 miles south
V Corp — 6 miles east
VI Corp — Manchester, Maryland
BIRNEY (2 Brigades) — Emmitsburg

Confederate

ANDERSON — 1½ miles west
HOOD — 4 miles west
McLAWS — 5 miles west
PICKETT — Chambersburg, Pa.

Longstreet's Confederates charge into the Wheatfield on the afternoon of July 2.

Hays and Avery's brigade attacking East Cemetery Hill on the evening of July 2.

Maj Gen Daniel Sickles, USA (LC)   *Lt Gen James Longstreet, CSA (NA)*

THE SECOND DAY
Thursday July 2, 1863

Major General George Gordon Meade, commander of the Union Army for less than a week, arrived at Gettysburg near midnight of July 1. After considerable inspection by moonlight, he concluded his position was weak, but unchangeable. Though his battered I and XI Corps had received reinforcements in the form of the XII Corps and portions of the III Corps, General *Lee's* Army was concentrating faster. Hancock's II Corps was close, but Sykes' V Corps was six miles away and Sedgewick's big VI Corps had only just begun its march from Manchester, Maryland, 35 miles away. An early morning assault could possibly knock the Union Army from Cemetery Ridge.

Meade, thinking an assault would be most likely on his right flank, had by six o'clock that morning, the entire XII Corps posted on Culps Hill and the adjoining ground to Rock Creek. The newly arriving units of the V Corps were being placed in reserve along the Baltimore Pike.

View from the south edge of the wheatfield. The monument and cannons in the center mark the position of Winslow's battery on the afternoon of July 2.

Geary's XII Corps division had been covering Little Round Top and its removal forced Sickles' III Corps to extend further to cover the position. The arrival of Hancock's II Corps eased Sickles' stretched line somewhat, but it placed the III Corps on the low ground between Cemetery Hill and Little Round Top. This low area was commanded by the high ground along the Emmitsburg Road and such a position was not to the arrogant Sickles' liking.

While Sickles' complained of his position to Meade's headquarters, the *Army of Northern Virginia* was preparing for the day's action. *Lee* knew the Union Army would probably not attack, and as he could not wait in hostile territory while his enemy grew stronger, he would have to take the initiative.

Instead of concentration as was *Lee's* usual strategy, his plan was to attack both wings of the Union Army. Three divisions, *Early*, *Rodes*, and *Johnson* were to attack the right; *Hood*, *McLaws*, and *Anderson's* Divisions would assault the left. The first three divisions, already in position, were to await the beginning of the latter three's attack for a combined assault on the Union flanks.

Hood and *McLaws* began their time consuming series of marches and countermarches about noon, already very late in the day. In an effort to disguise their flanking movement from the Union signal station on Little Round Top, precious time was lost. It was not until 3:30 PM that the Confederate *I* Corps troops were in position on Warfield Ridge. By then, the basic plan of attack had to be changed because of a movement made by a Union General, III Corps Commander Daniel Sickles.

ASSAULT ON THE UNION LEFT

Daniel Sickle's III Corps, holding the left flank of the army, was finding his position more and more precarious. By error, Buford's Cavalry Division, which was screening the Union left had been withdrawn and was sent to Westminster, Maryland. Sickles, with his screen gone, sent strong skirmishers out in the form of Berdan's Sharpshooters and the 3rd Maine regiment. They advanced beyond the Emmitsburg Road where they met units of *Wilcox's* Brigade of *Anderson's* Division in Pitzer's woods. After a sharp engagement, they withdrew and reported the encounter to Birney's Headquarters.

Though told repeatedly to hold his position by Headquarters, Sickles, upon hearing of the strong Confederate forces on his front, decided to occupy the high ground to the west. He ordered Birney's Division to advance along the southern flank and Humphrey's Division to move due west. The remainder of the Union line looked on in absolute disbelief.

General Birney first placed Ward's Brigade on the Devils Den hill to cover his left and deployed Grahams Brigade in the Peach Orchard along the Emmitsburg Road. DeTrobiand's Brigade did not deploy but remained in the area of the Wheatfield in column. He was to support either flank in the event of attack.

4:00 PM July 2, 1863 Two brigades of *Hood's* Confederate Division launched their attack against the southern salient of General Sickle's advanced III Corps line.

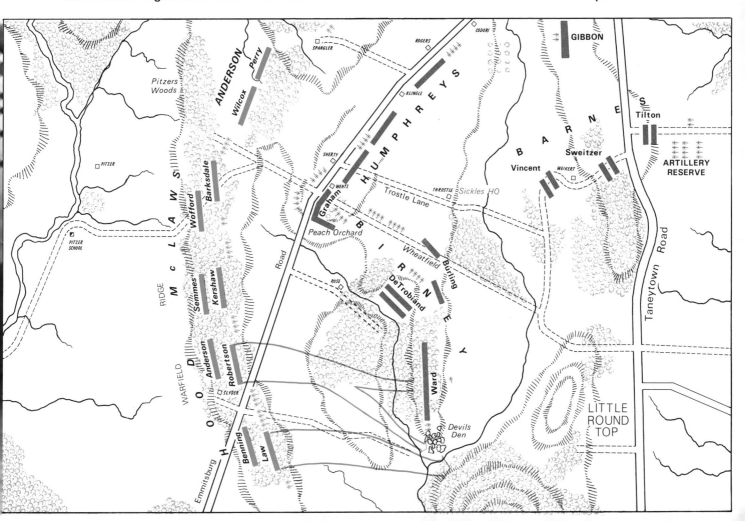

Humphrey's Division, linking up with Graham's Brigade, extended the line along the Emmitsburg Road nearly to the Codori Farm. Carr's Brigade held the first line, Brewster's Brigade held the second line. Burling's Brigade was detached from the division and used as Corps reserve, mostly as support for Birney's three brigades.

The higher ground of this new position was much better for the artillery but it had several distinct disadvantages. Primarily, as a V-shaped line, it exposed two sides to an enemy attack and was likely to be crushed in a vice. Also both fronts were facing thick woods, easily concealing large enemy forces.

The main fault was the sheer distances involved. Sickles simply did not have sufficient forces to cover such a long defensive line. Because of this, Little Round Top had to be left unoccupied and a large gap allowed to exist between Humphrey's right and Gibbon's left of the II Corps. The III Corps was hanging alone in the face of superior Southern forces.

Sickles completed the Corps' movement about 3 o'clock. He rode off to Army Headquarters to find General Meade greatly displeased. Before leaving with Sickles to inspect this new position, Meade ordered the V Corps to begin moving to support of the left. The arriving units of the big VI Corps would remain to support the right.

General Meade, on seeing the III Corps' position, saw it at once to be inadequate. Sickles offered to withdraw, but by now the skirmish and artillery firing along the fronts was becoming intense. Withdrawal would not be possible. Meade at once authorized a full division from the II Corps and the entire V Corps to reinforce the III Corps line.

LITTLE ROUND TOP

At 4:00 PM, General John *Hood's* Division of Longstreet's Corps, began their attack on the southern front of the III Corps salient. *Hood*, who had been preoccupied with Little Round Top, sought to have the attack orders changed to make it the objective but failed. He did, however, order *Law's* Brigade on the extreme right of his division to bear still further to the right and attack that key point. With *Robertson's* Brigade on their left and *Anderson's* and *Benning's* Brigades following in support, *Law* moved out at double time for Little Round Top.

Hood's line of attack centered on Ward's Brigade, deployed along the hill above Devils Den. Smith's New York Battery, covered the left of Ward's line and steadily poured case and shell into *Law* and *Robertson*. *Robertson* hit Ward's front line and carried the position, but *Law's* Brigade, in sweeping past Devils Den into Plum Run gorge, carried two of *Robertson's* regiments with him. Undermanned and unsupported, the remaining two regiments found themselves flanked

General John Hood's Confederate Division charged from this line against Union positions at Devils Den and on Little Round Top, seen in the distance.

by Detrobiand's 17th Maine and were forced to fall back. Ward's men then surged forward and recaptured their former positions.

Law's Brigade, advancing in a wide arc, swept aside the three Union regiments defending the valley in front of Little Round Top. Law's right flank, the 15th Alabama, pushed up Big Round Top on the western face and crossed over, descending into the vale between the round tops. Little Round Top might have been occupied easily if it were not for the foresight of General Warren.

Brigadier General Gouvernor Warren, Chief Engineer of the Union Army, saw the strategic importance of Little Round Top while at the signal station on its summit. He saw too that the III Corps could not possibly defend it and that its loss would flank the entire Union line. He set out at once to gather forces for its defense.

Warren could see the brigades of the V Corps moving in from the Taneytown Road and rode to meet them. At the Weikert house, Warren stopped Vincent's Brigade, and with General Barnes' permission, detached it for use on Little Round Top. At double time, the brigade rushed up the northern slope and over the crest. It arrived not a minute too soon.

Smith's New York Battery of four 10-pound Parrotts held the extreme left of Sickle's line above Devils Den. Three guns were captured later in the day by Benning's Confederate Brigade.

Law's right flank, the *15th Alabama*, moved across the valley and onto the slopes of Little Round Top, running headlong into the 20th Maine. The remainder of *Law's* line made contact and the Battle for Little Round Top was on. A desperate struggle hand to hand among the scattered boulders developed; attacks and counterattacks were launched and repulsed. The little valley became a virtual slaughterhouse.

The terrain of the hill favored the defenders, but the large number of Confederates were becoming difficult to contain on Vincent's right. *Robertson's* two detached regiments were rapidly approaching the top. Hazlett's battery had arrived, and although unable to depress their barrels to aid Vincent, their morale value sparked the Union forces.

General Warren, still busy gathering forces, stopped Weed's Brigade of Ayre's Division on the march and directed it to Little Round Top. The 140th New York regiment, leading this brigade, arrived on the crest as the Texan regiments were nearing the top. Still in column, the 140th New York charged into the Confederates, throwing them back down the hill. In the bloody struggle, Colonel O'Rorke, the regimental commander was killed along with 133 casualties of his gallant regiment. But they had saved the Union right on Little Round Top.

On the left of Vincent's line, the *15th Alabama* was still battering away at the 20th Maine, making little headway against the smaller Union regiment. The Maine boys, after making a heroic stand, finished up by counterattacking the *15th Alabama* and repulsed them.

Law's forces had now suffered many casualties and had lost its momentum against mounting Union forces. One final charge after dark was turned back, convincing *Law* that further attempts were hopeless. The brigade and its two detached regiments fell back to Devils Den, now in Confederate hands.

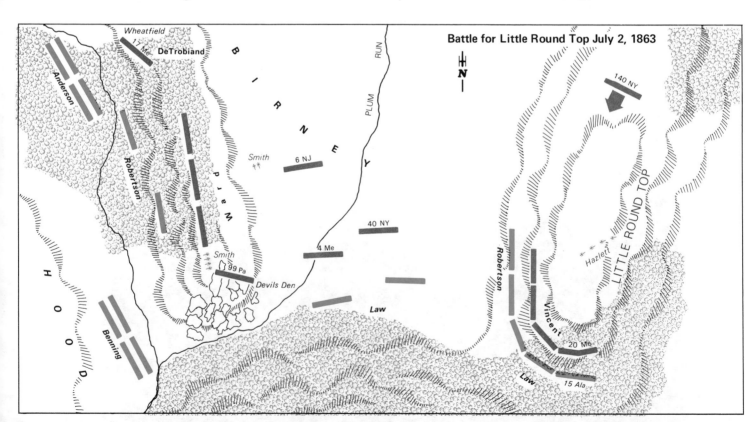

Battle for Little Round Top July 2, 1863

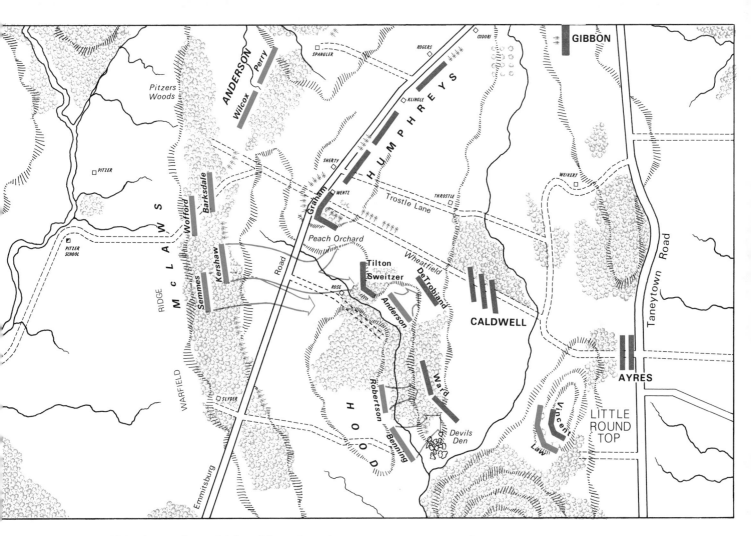

5:00 PM July 2, 1863 The Confederate brigades of *Kershaw* and *Semmes* attacked the Union positions in the Peach Orchard and Wheatfield.

DEVILS DEN AND THE WHEATFIELD

Robertson's two regiments that remained in front of the Devils Den hill were in serious trouble. Repulsed by Ward and Detrobiand, the regiments fell back and called for support from General *Hood*. *Hood* though, had been seriously wounded in the arm, and as the senior Brigadier, General *Law* should have taken command. Since he was in advance of the division at Little Round Top, no one immediately took command of the division.

By sheer luck though, *Benning's* Brigade suddenly appeared opposite Devils Den by following the sound of battle through the thick smoke that covered the field. Moving without orders from reserve, four regiments of *Anderson's* Brigade suddenly turned up on *Robertson's* left. Now Ward and Detrobiand found themselves in serious trouble.

Robertson and *Benning* joined forces and attacked the Devils Den, smashing the left of Ward's line and capturing three of Smith's four 10-pound Parrotts. Reinforcements failed to halt the Confederate drive and the Union forces

47

surrendered Devils Den. *Anderson's* Brigade, striking at Detrobiand's center in the Wheatfield, pushed them back to the northern end. Although the III Corps southern flank had crumbled, help was beginnning to arrive.

The II Corps Division ordered on the field earlier by Meade was General John Caldwell's First Division. Forming at the northern end of the Wheatfield, they passed through Detrobiand's retreating troops and charged *Anderson's* Brigade. The V Corps Brigades of Tilton and Sweitzer had already moved into the woods west of the Wheatfield in the area now known as the Loop. Appearing on *Anderson's* flank and coupled with Caldwell's advance, they forced the Confederate brigade back through the Wheatfield.

Now the Second Division of *Longstreet's* Corps commanded by General *Lafayette McLaw's* began to move in support of *Hood*. *Kershaw's* Brigade, followed closely by *Semmes'* Brigade, advanced out of their cover along Warfield Ridge. Marching by way of the Rose house, *Kershaw's* line divided and struck the southern flank of the Peach Orchard and the Tilton-Sweitzer position in the area of the Loop.

But *Kershaw*, suddenly met by the advance of Caldwell's Division on his right and strong artillery on his left, was forced back onto *Semmes*. Tilton and Sweitzer, thinking Caldwell's men were replacements, withdrew, leaving Colonel Zook's Brigade exposed. *Kershaw* and *Semmes* renewed the attack and forced the Union Brigades again to retreat and yield the Wheatfield. Colonel Cross' Brigade, sent into the melee on the Devils Den hill to join Ward, was threatened on the flank and rear.

By now, the scattered Union regiments of three different Corps were fighting a costly unco-ordinated battle. General Caldwell, seeing no overall commander, quickly ordered his reserve brigade of Brooke's, supported by Sweitzer and two brigades of Ayre's Division of regulars, to attack. The line charged back across the Wheatfield and into the woods beyond, carrying the Confederate line with it through the blood-stained wheat. Day's and Burbank's regulars joined the remnants of Ward, Burling, and Cross holding the rise east of the Wheatfield. Once again, the Union position was stable.

And once again *McLaws* destroyed it. Ordering his last two brigades to the attack, *Barksdale* and *Wofford* advanced on the exposed flanks of the Peach Orchard. Defended only by Graham's reinforced brigade, the Union line could not hold under the pressure.

Wofford's advance carried him through the Peach Orchard, eastwardly to the woods previously held by Tilton and Sweitzer. This placed them square on the flank and rear of the entire Union line southeast of the Wheatfield.

Nearly surrounded now, Brooke and Sweitzer fell back diagonally across the Wheatfield, fighting for every inch. The combat was virtually hand to hand. Colonel Sweitzer's horse was shot from under him, even the crown of his hat was split open by a bullet. Colonel Jeffords of the 4th Michigan was bayoneted. The losses were enormous. Ayre's regulars, caught in the murderous crossfires, retreated in perfect order through the inferno. Casualties mounted, Colonel Cross was killed, Colonel Zook mortally wounded, Brooke was wounded. The Wheatfield was littered with thousands of dead and dying of both sides. Before long, the Union retreat became a complete rout.

Barksdale's Mississippi Brigade, after crushing Graham's Brigade, pressed on toward the Trostle Farm. General Sickles, whose headquarters were at that farm, was severely wounded in the leg and carried from the field. Everywhere, retreating batteries and regiments fled toward Plum Run and Little Round Top. The entire III Corps salient had given way.

THE SALIENT CRUSHED

General Andrew Humphrey's Division, strung thinly along the Emmitsburg Road, found itself in a very dangerous position. Flanked and passed by *Barksdale's* Brigade on the left, *Anderson's* Division of *Hill's* Corps was now advancing on his front. *Wilcox's* and *Perry's* Brigade, with *Wright's* Brigade on the left, were moving strongly toward Humphrey's over-streched lines.

6:00 PM July 2, 1863 Union positions along the Emmitsburg Road were heavily assaulted by Confederate brigades, forcing the collapse of the entire Union salient.

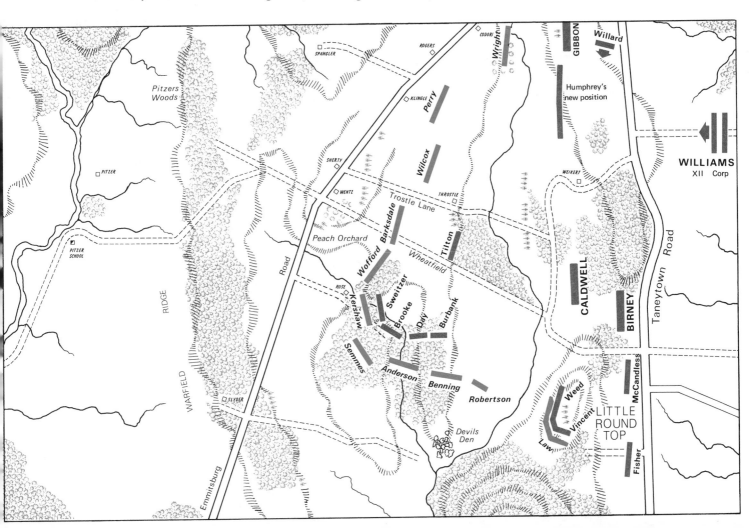

General Humphrey, wishing to move forward and meet his attackers, nevertheless heeded his orders and began a withdrawal. Under heavy fire, Humphrey's men marched back in order, turning to fire, then marching again. Humphrey constantly exposed himself to fire to encourage his men and prevent a rout. By the time they reached Cemetery Ridge on Gibbon's left, hundreds of fallen comrades marked their line of march.

Even with Humphrey's Division in position, a huge gap still existed between his left and Little Round Top. It was towards this gap that *Barksdale* and *Wilcox* were headed. If they broke through here, the Union Army would be cut in two and the Taneytown Road lost. Destruction of the Army of the Potomac was almost certain to follow.

Thrown into this gap was a collection of scattered units. Colonel McGilvery gathered together batteries and random guns to form a line of about 15 cannons along the east bank of Plum Run. By intensive use of canister, McGilvery succeeded in holding off *Barksdale's* presistent brigade until Willard's II Corps Brigade arrived. Colonel Willard charged with his New York regiments into the flank of *Barksdale's* Brigade, throwing them into disorder. General *William Barksdale* fell mortally wounded while trying to rally his retreating troops and his opponent, Colonel Willard, also fell dying among his brigade's many casualties.

Arriving from Culp's Hill, elements of the XII Corps began to deploy in support of McGilvery's line. Lockwood's independent Brigade, led momentarily by General Meade himself, charged into the woods opposite McGilvery and carried their attack nearly to the Emmitsburg Road. Upon Lockwood's return, the XII Corps was quickly ordered back to the almost undefended Culp's Hill where a Confederate attack was under way.

The three brigades of *Anderson's* Division, advancing on *Barksdale's* left, were moving against Humphrey's retreating Division and the gap existing between him and McGilvery's Artillery. *Wright's* Brigade, on the left of *Anderson's* line, first struck the two regiments sent out by Gibbons at the Codori house. Though expecting support on his left from *Posey* and *Mahone*, *Wright* continued to advance without it and attacked Gibbon's front. Webb's Brigade quickly counterattacked. Without support on either flank, *Wright* withdrew from Cemetery Ridge.

Wilcox's Brigade, moving unopposed toward Humphrey's exposed left, was seen by General Hancock. Looking around for any available troops, he halted the 1st Minnesota of Harrow's Brigade. Knowing the danger, he ordered this single regiment to stop *Wilcox's* entire brigade. Attacking without question, the 1st Minnesota charged them and succeeded in stopping the brigade cold. The cost was terrible. The regiment suffered 82% casualties, the highest among any regiment on the North American continent. They alone, perhaps, had saved the Union line.

50

View from Little Round Top towards Plum Run Valley.

Perry's Florida Brigade struck the now prepared division of Humphrey's. Angered by their costly retreat, the division suddenly counterattacked and caused *Perry* to fall back before their determined attack. Union reinforcements began pouring into the lines. Doubleday's and Robinson's Divisions of the I Corps arrived. Stannard's Brigade of Doubleday's Division joined the counterattack. The Union lines now exploded with advancing Union regiments.

At Little Round Top, McCandless' Brigade charged into the massed Confederates and drove them back across the Wheatfield. Stopping at the stone wall on the east side of the field, McCandless received the support of Nevin's and Bartlett's VI Corps Brigades. They spent the night at this forward position.

The counterattacks, coupled with the darkness, succeeded in convincing the Confederates that the Union lines were again strong. Many abandoned guns were recovered and over 600 Confederate prisoners were taken. The line seemed at last secure.

The VI Corps Brigades that moved in behind Little Round Top were now used to patch the line and provide reserves. The 20th Maine advanced up Big Round Top and cleared it for occupation by Fisher's V Corps Brigade. Russell's and Grant's Brigade covered the left rear east of the round tops. Caldwell's battered division went into the line aside Doubleday, and what remained of the III Corps was placed in reserve along the Taneytown Road.

Though organized fighting ceased, skirmishing and sniping continued. The howls and screams of the thousands of wounded added to the terror of the night. The battle was long and fierce, but equally indecisive. Indecisive too, was the battle raging on the right of the Union line at Culp's and Cemetery Hill.

Maj Gen Henry Slocum, USA (LC)   *Maj Gen Edward Johnson, CSA (LC)*

CULP'S HILL

The plan prepared by General *Lee* calling for *Ewell's* attack to synchronize with *Longstreet's* went astray from the start. Either by atmospheric conditions or inattention or both, *Longstreet's* furious artillery duel went unnoticed. It was not until *Hill's* cannons opened up to support *Anderson's* Division did *Ewell* realize that the attack on the left was under way. Actually, it had been going on for well over an hour.

Ewell, now aware he was to attack, still did not give the order. Earlier in the afternoon, an erroneous report of Union troops out the York Pike prompted *Early* to send *Gordon's* and *Smith's* Brigades out the road in hot pursuit of a non-existent enemy. Being short by two brigades, *Ewell* could not send troops into action without a substantial reserve.

Nearing six o'clock, the reported Union troops turned out to be the Union Cavalry screen and with the recent arrival of *Stuart's* Cavalry they could be contained. In any event, *Smith's* Brigade remained to assist *Stuart* and only *Gordon's* Brigade returned to *Early's* command.

Although still short a full brigade, *Ewell* could wait no longer. He at once ordered General *Edward Johnson's* entire division to move against the Culp's Hill positions. The Union XII Corps, holding these positions from the summit to Rock Creek, was at that very moment being withdrawn from the defensive works. By General Meade's order, the entire Corps save Greene's Brigade, was being hurriedly sent to assist the crumbling Union left. This movement was well under way by the time *Johnson* began his advance.

General George Greene's Brigade had been holding the extreme right of the Corps and was dug in on the summit. As the remainder of the Corps pulled out, Greene began extending his right to occupy the vacated breastworks. He barely got the movement started before *Johnson's* men were swarming up the hill.

Jones' Brigade was first to strike and did so square in Greene's center as *Steuart's* and *Walker's* Brigades were moving around his already extended right. Greene's center was solidly entrenched among the boulders and trees of the summit and they delivered a terrible fire on *Jones'* scattered assault. The trees and rocks broke up his attack and approaching darkness made movement difficult. *Nicholl's* Brigade relieved *Jones*, but even his fresh troops could not budge the stubborn New Yorkers.

With *Steuart* and *Walker* it was an entirely different matter. They moved virtually unopposed into the Union trenches abandoned less than an hour before

Evening, July 2, 1863 Successful Confederate attacks against Culp's and Cemetery Hill were later nullified because of *Ewell's* failure to exploit this advantage.

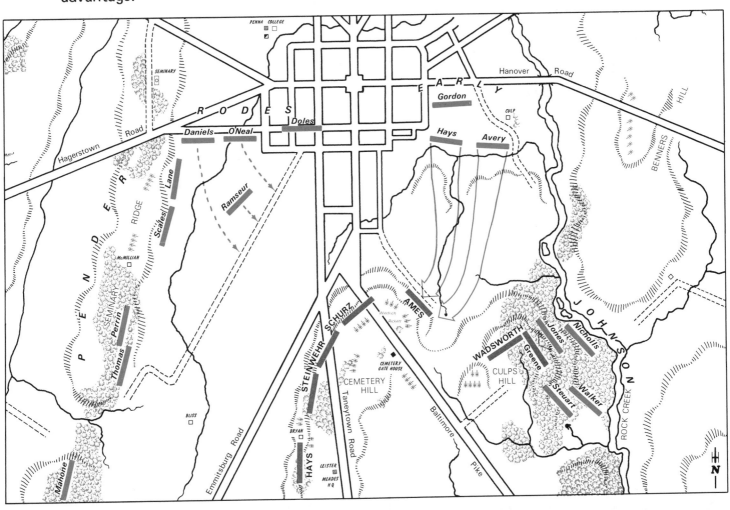

Battery on East Cemetery Hill, looking towards Stevens Knoll.

by Colgrove and McDougall. At this point, only a handfull of Union troops were between them and the Baltimore Pike. The capture of this road would have been a severe, perhaps fatal, blow to Meade, but only the skirmishers continued to advance. The main body of Confederate troops remained in the captured trenches. Darkness had made them too cautious.

While the fighting raged along the summit, Greene had been reinforced by several regiments from the I and II Corps. General John Geary's Division, who had become lost in its search for the Union left and was returning without finding it, arrived just in time to halt *Steuart's* skirmishers. With *Nicholl's* last assault on the summit repulsed, the first battle for Culp's Hill came to a close.

CEMETERY HILL

After finally ordering *Johnson's* Division to the attack, *Ewell* then turned attention to *Early's* and *Rodes'* Divisions and the assault against Cemetery Hill. *Early's* Division was to attack East Cemetery Hill and *Rodes* to attack up the western side. Caught in such a vice, the Union I and XI Corps could be crushed. This operation had an excellent chance of success, but the poor co-operation that plagued *Ewell's* Corps was still very apparent.

At dusk, General *Early* formed the brigades of *Hays* and *Avery* in the fields near the Culp house. In neat rows, they marched over the rise into full view of the artillery on Cemetery Hill and Stevens Knoll. Immediately, a shower of shot and shell began its grim work, Colonel *Avery* being one of the first to fall. But the North Carolinans and Louisannans steadily advanced. In the dim light, the brilliant muzzle flashes of the Union artillery sparkled along the crest.

Along the base of East Cemetery Hill, Barlow's old XI Corps Division was entrenched. These Union troops had little stomach for a fight after the previous days encounter with *Early's* men. One charge easily pierced their line. With the momentum of the attack, the Confederate wave surged up the slopes on the heels of the retreating XI Corps troops. Before anyone fully realized, they found themselves among the cannons of Ricketts and Wiedrich's Batteries on the crest. The Confederates had taken East Cemetery Hill.

In the darkness, it sounded to *Rodes* as if Cemetery Hill had erupted. His brigades had not been prepared to attack and he was now reluctant to do so. *Early's* insistence prompted him to move his assault force into the sunken road south of the town, but no further. His skirmish line advanced but halted when met by a show of force by Union artillery. Actually, Steinwehr and Schurz had dangerously stripped their positions and *Rodes'* attack would surely have met with success. General *Early* knowing *Rodes'* attack would not come, could not release his only reserve, *Gordon's* Brigade. *Hays* and *Avery* would not be supported.

On the slim beachhead of Cemetery Hill, the Confederates still held gamely. Reinforcements were pouring into the Union lines from all commands and converging on that half circle that was Southern territory. Carroll's Brigade from the II Corps and several regiments from the I Corps swelled the Union forces. In the darkness, the Confederates kept their fire to a minimum to avoid firing on *Rodes'* men who were to appear at any moment. Still, in the intermittent flashes of light, only rank upon rank of blue could be seen.

After repulsing several determined attacks, the two gallant brigades finally were forced to fall back or be captured. They did not retreat in disorder, but yielded the ground foot by foot. But the fact is they did yield, and did so from a position that if they could have held, would have been in position to wreck the entire Union line. The cost of the failure was high, over 600 Confederate casualties.

Cemetery Hill could have been the blow that broke the Union Army's back. Because of *Rodes'* failure to attack and *Early's* inability to support *Hays* and *Avery*, this vital position could not be held. Seven Southern brigades were available for this operation but only two brigades went into action. Victory was never again as close as it was during that hour. This then was truely the High Water Mark of the Confederacy.

SUMMARY—SECOND DAY

The second day was not as decisive as it could have been. Confederate forces had attacked nearly every segment of the Union line, but always a little late, a little too hesitant, and much too unco-ordinated. Victory was always just out of reach.

Confederate forces carried the field but failed to pull out a real victory. Casualties were not too severe but any amount was difficult for them to replace. *Pickett's* Division was newly arrived and fresh and part of *Anderson's* and *Pender's* Divisions had not been used. Both armies had plenty of fight left for still another day of slaughter.

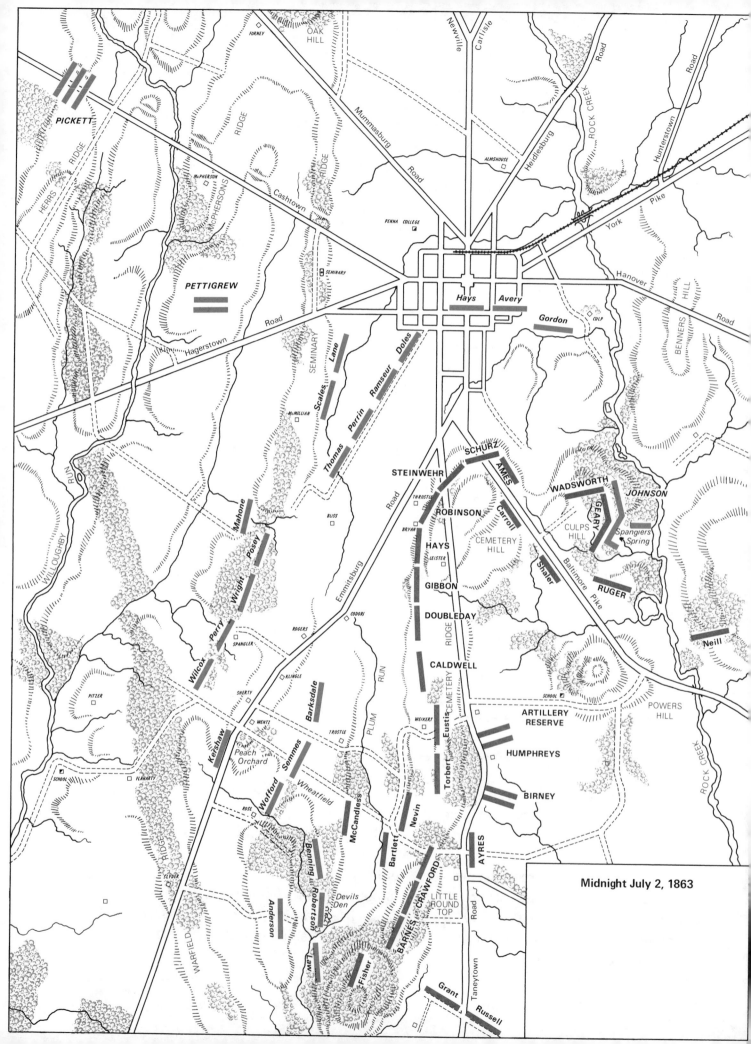

PICKETT

PETTIGREW

FORNEY

OAK HILL

McPHERSON

HERRS RIDGE

McPHERSONS RIDGE

Cashtown Road

Hagerstown Road

SEMINARY RIDGE

SEMINARY

Mahone

Posey

Wright

Perry

Wilcox

PITZER

WILLOUGHBY RUN

SPANGLER

SHERFY

KERSHAW

Peach Orchard

SCHOOL

FLAHARTY

Semmes

Wofford

WENTZ

ROSE

Barksdale

TROSTLE

Wheatfield

McCandless

Benning

Robertson

Anderson

Law

SLYDER

Devils Den

Fisher

BARNES

CRAWFORD

Bartlett

Nevin

PLUM RUN

WEIKERT

Torbert

Eustis

LITTLE ROUND TOP

CEMETERY RIDGE

Grant

Russell

McMILLIAN

PENNA COLLEGE

BLISS

Scales

Lane

Thomas

Perrin

Ramseur

Doles

Emmitsburg Road

THROSTLE

BRYAN

CODORI

ROGERS

KLINGLE

STEINWEHR

SCHURZ

ROBINSON

HAYS

LEISTER

GIBBON

DOUBLEDAY

CALDWELL

AYRES

HUMPHREYS

BIRNEY

ARTILLERY RESERVE

SCHOOL

AMES

Carroll

CEMETERY HILL

Shaler

RUGER

CULPS HILL

GEARY

Spangler's Spring

WADSWORTH

JOHNSON

POWERS HILL

Neill

Hays

Avery

Gordon

CULP

ALMSHOUSE

Mummasburg Road

Heidlesburg Road

Carlisle Road

Newville Road

Hunterstown Road

ROCK CREEK

Road

York Pike

Hanover Road

BENNERS HILL

Baltimore Pike

ROCK CREEK

Taneytown Road

Midnight July 2, 1863

Maj Gen Winfield Hancock, USA (LC)   *Maj Gen George Pickett, CSA (NA)*

THE THIRD DAY
Friday July 3, 1863

Dawn broke on this Friday with promises of a hot, sultry day. The birds that remained on the field chirped and cheerfully searched for food among the dead and wounded. In the shattered Peach Orchard and elsewhere, they dutifully fed their young.

Men awoke to their songs in both battle lines and shuffled to prepare for another day..In Union Army Headquarters, a vote of Corps Commanders the night before had decided its course. They would stay and fight but would not take a major offensive.

On the Confederate side, there was little choice. General *Lee* had to either take the offensive or retreat, and he could not retreat in light of the two previous days. *Lee* was convinced only a final knockout blow would destroy the Army of the Potomac once and for all.

General *Lee* knew that because of his attacks on the Union flanks the day before, the Union Army must be heavy there and weak in the center. This was where he planned to hit Meade and cut the Union Army in two, destroying it then at leisure.

Lee's plan was not without its dangers. First, he had only one fresh division, that of General *Pickett* numbering about 4,500 men. Secondly, General *Longstreet* opposed the plan and favored an attack around the Union left flank. Third, nearly a mile of open ground separated the two lines at that point.

The morning's planning was interrupted by heavy musket firing in the area of Culp's Hill. *Lee* was puzzled as to Meade's intentions but guessed it was only an attempt to dislodge *Johnson's* men from around Spangler's Spring. This was exactly the reason.

Meade had voted too for the policy of no offensive but was forced to order the XII Corps to clean out the Confederates threatening the Baltimore Pike. Slocum's Corps, during the night, had hemmed in *Johnson's* Division and now attacked to recapture their trenches.

Johnson's Division had been reinforced during the night by two brigades from *Rodes'* Division and one from *Early's*. The reason being that *Lee* expected to use the area in co-ordination with *Longstreet's* attack on the Union center.

In the area of Spangler's Spring a stiff fight raged. Colgrove sent the 2nd Massachusetts and the 27th Indiana against the earthworks north of the spring but they suffered frightening losses. They fell back but successfully repulsed a Confederate counterattack.

McDougall's Brigade attacked *Steuart* with some success, though gains were small. On Culp's Hill, the Confederates again were assaulting the summit, but

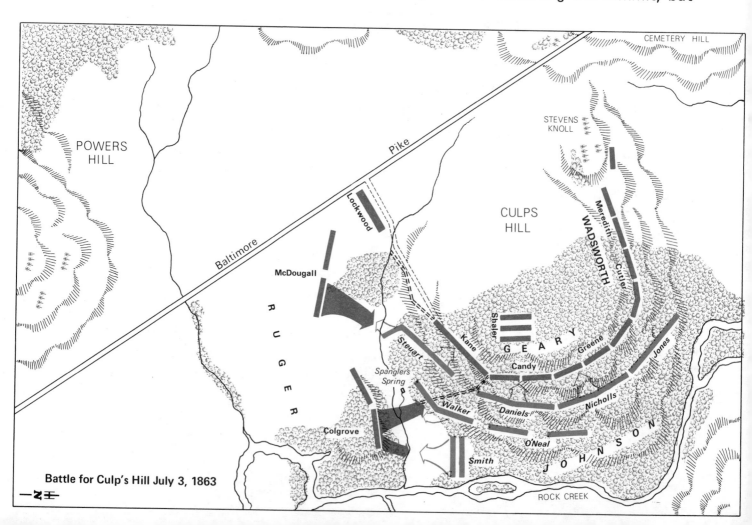

Battle for Culp's Hill July 3, 1863

Greene's men still held. Candy's Brigade, then Kane's troops repulsed swarms of attacking Confederates. Finally, in one great counterattack, the Confederate lines gave way. The Union troops surged forward and captured the works. With the fight knocked out of them, *Johnson* withdrew his command beyond Rock Creek. The battle for Culp's Hill was over.

With *Johnson* in no position to assist, *Longstreet* liked the plan even less. *Lee* was concerned, but decided to add *Heth* and *Pender's* old divisions to make up for the loss of this diversion. *Longstreet* still did not like it but ordered *Pickett* into position in front of Spangler's Woods. *Heth's* Division under *Pettigrew* and *Pender's* under *Trimble* moved into the woods along Seminary Ridge directly opposite the clump of trees that was the aim point of the attack.

For most of the morning, the Confederate artillery was deploying along the high ground running north from the Peach Orchard. By noontime about twenty batteries were aimed at Cemetery Ridge. The stage was set for one of the greatest cannonades in the history of the war.

Most reliable sources place the commencement of the firing at one o'clock. Whatever time it was, the Confederate artillery line erupted in smoke and fire, hurling shells into the somewhat surprised Union line. Union artillery did not

Pickett's Charge Advancing from their cover along Seminary Ridge, the Confederate wave surged toward Cemetery Ridge.

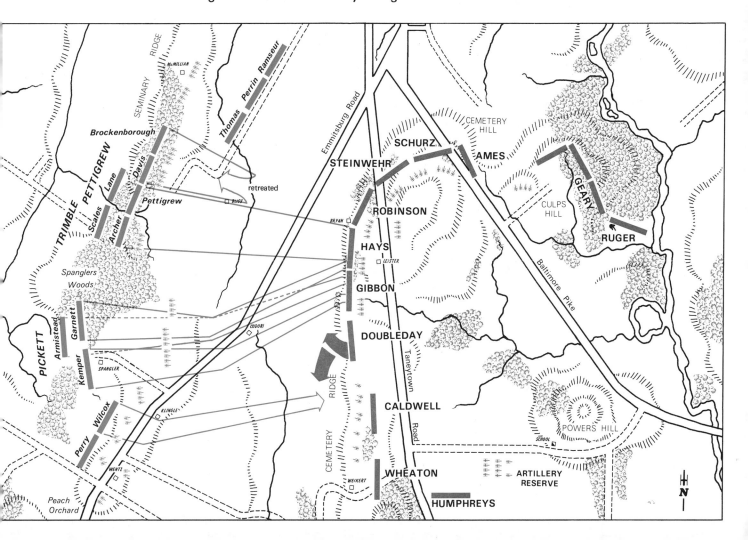

return fire for 10 to 15 minutes on orders from General Hunt so as to conserve ammunition. Only General Hancock countermanded the order for his batteries for reasons of infantry morale.

After ten minutes, it became apparent it was not to be just harassing artillery fire. The Confederates had brought up over a hundred guns and all were steadily pouring a deadly rain on the Union line without respite.

Union artillery had started returning fire but the batteries along Cemetery Ridge were exposed and suffering heavy losses in men and horses. Union batteries further south along the ridge and on Little Round Top had better cover and their fire started to take an equally heavy toll on the concealed Confederate infantry. Though unintentional, the shells that were overshooting the artillery were landing in the midst of *Longstreet's* attack force.

Confederate guns also were firing high as shells streamed over Cemetery Ridge causing damage among the wagons and hospitals in the rear areas. General Meade's Headquarters, located behind the focal point of the Confederate fire, became a hell-hole of bursting shells and dying men and horses. At the height of the barrage, Meade was forced to vacate his headquarters and move to safer facilities on Power's Hill.

The main purpose of the Confederate cannonade was to wreck the Union batteries defending the point of attack. Colonel *Alexander*, who commanded the *I* Corps artillery, had the authority to determine if this was accomplished. In effect, an artillery Colonel had the responsibility of launching a massive infantry assault.

Nearing three o'clock, the two hour cannonade was causing visual damage on the Union line. Colonel *Alexander* observed that Union batteries on Cemetery Ridge were pulling out. This was the omen he required. He immediately sent word to General *Longstreet* that the time was right to strike.

What he observed and what was actually occurring were not one and the same. The Union batteries were indeed withdrawing, but only to replenish their empty cassions. Replacement batteries from reserve were at that moment moving to take their place in the line. *Longstreet's* troops would not be going against weakened Union artillery.

Nevertheless, the Confederate troops rose up and formed their lines. All along Seminary Ridge, from Spangler's Woods to the McMillian house, Confederate troops straightened their ranks and moved forward. In perfect order, nearly 11,000 men surged forth with uncased colors leading their regiments.

The cannonade began to fade off, and the Union troops knew what to expect. Infantry! Men who dared peek over the stone walls were greeted by a sight many had never seen before. From the woods to their front, *Trimble's* and *Pettigrew's* Divisions flowed from the trees in a line half a mile long. Further to the left, over the rise in front of Spangler's Woods, came the three brigades of *Pickett's* Division. Many of the Union troops were simply awestruck.

60

The Hall-Harrow Line. This section of the Union line was struck by Pickett's Division on the afternoon of July 3. The single tree in the center marks the angle.

Awestruck or not, Union artillery began its deadly job of reducing the advancing ranks. *Pickett's* Division on the right and *Davis'* and *Brockenborough's* Brigades on the left were taking severe losses from the artillery firing on their flanks. *Pickett's* men weathered the storm of shells well, executing oblique movements and dressing ranks as if on a parade field. But *Davis* and *Brockenborough*, unable to take the heavy fire from Cemetery Hill, broke ranks at the burning Bliss barn and retreated back to Seminary Ridge. A blemish on an otherwise excellent advance.

The attacking line narrowed as it approached the Emmitsburg Road. Fences hindered their advance but lines halted to dress ranks and move out again. Crossing the road, the ground now sloped up to the clump of trees. Troops began to double-time and the rebel yell could be heard along the moving mass of men. Union firing now increased to a furious tempo. Artillery and muskets blazed at the Confederates charging up the slope. The climax was now close at hand.

Weakened by the incessant rain of artillery shells, the Union infantry's firing began to break up the charge. Groups reached the stone walls and crossed them but were met by double canister from the waiting batteries. Whole companies were mowed down like ripened wheat.

The last 200 yards. Pickett's men charged up this slope and broke the Union line along the stone wall. The clump of trees was much larger then and the remaining small grove marks the furtherest advance of Confederate troops.

The Angle The Confederate assault pierced the Union line only to be met by fierce resistance on their front and flanks.

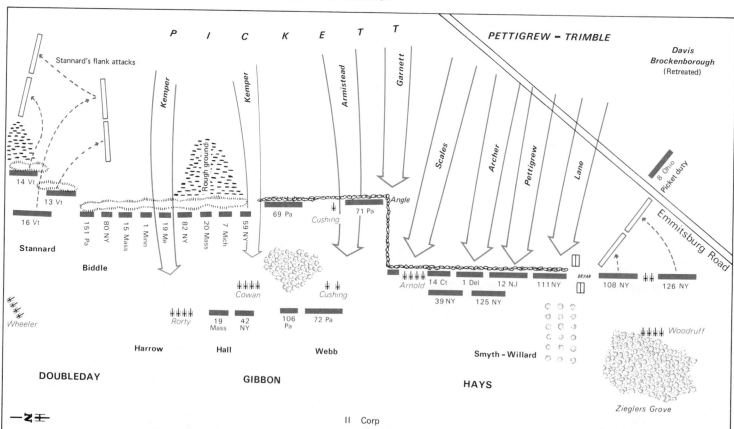

Inside the angle. Confederate troops broke through and silenced Cushing's Battery of 3-inch guns. The scroll monument marks the spot where Confederate General Armistead fell leading the charge.

The Confederate assault now took the shape of a triangle, with the apex at the clump of trees. The vulnerable sides came under heavy flank attack, first from Stannard's Vermont Brigade on the southern side, then by scattered regiments on the north. The tactic of double envelopment had occured. The attack was being neatly contained in a box.

General *Armistead* led a group of 200 men into the angle to capture Cushing's annoying guns. The bitter hand to hand fighting resulted in *Armistead's* death and the small group's repulsion. The attack had been broken and retreat began from Cemetery Ridge.

General *Lee* had watched the brave assault sweep to its climax and recede. He rode into the fields to rally his beaten troops and to have them prepare for a Union counterattack he was sure would follow. To General *Wilcox* he said, "The fault is mine."

Meade and the Army of the Potomac was badly shaken by the bold assault. The VI Corps was available for a counterattack, but Meade was too cautious to throw away victory now. He knew only too well that *Lee's* men still had plenty of fight.

Night came and with it a pleasant respite from the heat. *Lee* ordered his lines pulled back in the event of a morning attack. Culp's Hill and the town were evacuated by *Ewell* and *Longstreet* pulled his troops from the Wheatfield and Devils Den area. The line on July 4 ran along Seminary Ridge from Oak Hill to beyond the Peach Orchard. It rained all day that Saturday, and in its cover, *Lee* began his retreat.

Maj Gen David Gregg, USA (LC)　　　*Maj Gen J.E.B. Stuart, CSA (LC)*

CAVALRY BATTLE

One of the least visited areas of the Gettysburg Military Park sadly enough is the East Cavalry Battlefield. Located about 2½ miles east on the Hanover Road, its distance from the centers of attraction forces it to take a secondary place.

But here, on the afternoon of July 3, 1863, the Union cavalry of General David Gregg stopped *J.E.B. Stuart's* Confederate cavalry from turning the right flank and attacking Meade's rear.

Lee's plan called for *Stuart's* flanking movement to harass Meade's communications and, if *Pickett* was successful, to participate in the rout. With three brigades of cavalry and one of mounted infantry, *Stuart* had positioned his force along Cress Ridge by about 2:30 PM.

Skirmishing began immediately with the Union cavalrymen of McIntosh's brigade in plain view to their front. Artillery then joined and a sharp engagement ensued.

Stuart's force numbered 6,000 troopers against only two brigades of Gregg's division. But General George Custer's brigade, detached from Kilpatrick's cavalry division, was nearby and was only too happy to join in the expected fight. This brought the Union saber to 5,000 men with a good edge in artillery.

The Confederate cavalry moved from the woods in perfect order. With drawn sabers, they advanced steadily despite a tremendous rifle and artillery fire tearing holes in their ranks.

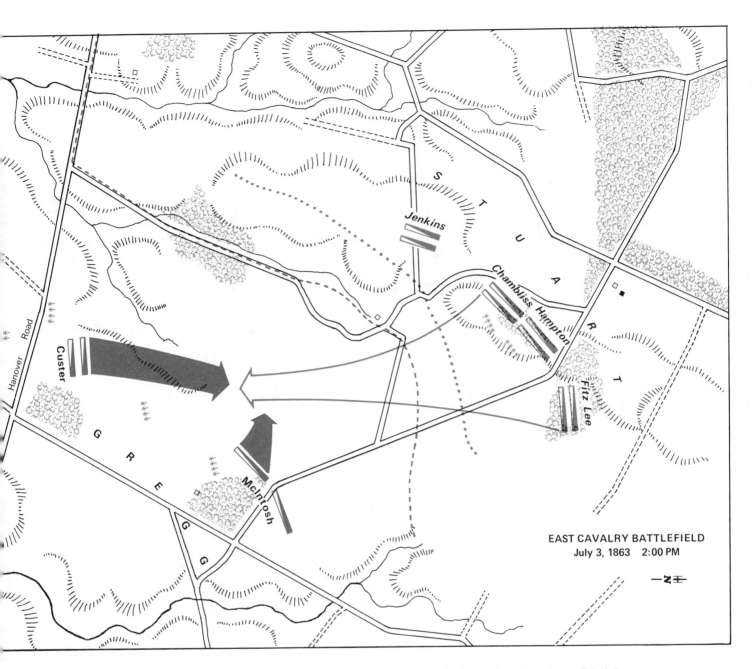

East Cavalry Field, July 3, 1863 General David Gregg's Cavalry Division intercepted *J.E.B. Stuart's* Confederate Cavalry and defeated it in an epic cavalry fight.

Custer's brigade was also in column, and seeing a chance for glory, he ordered his brigade of Michigan cavalry to charge. Across the field with flashing sabers, Custer led the attack into the ranks of *Hampton's* brigade. Charges and countercharges were launched and repulsed.

Stuart's men met the attack well, but during the course of the struggle Gregg began hitting his flanks and *Stuart* found one of his brigades extremely low on ammunition. Hard pressed by a determined enemy, *Stuart* had little choice but to break off the action. His troopers fell back to the woods and waited until dark. Upon hearing of *Pickett's* repulse, he withdrew his cavalry to Seminary Ridge.

EPILOGUE

Gettysburg had truly earned its place as the climatic battle of the Civil War. Coupled with the surrender of Vicksburg the very next day, the curtain began to close on the Confederacy. The loss of Vicksburg was severe enough but the defeat at Gettysburg was the fatal blow.

There was little doubt that Gettysburg was a Union victory. In three days of hard fighting, *Lee* was unable to dislodge the Federal troops from their positions. After two years of consistent victories, Gettysburg smashed the image of Southern invincibility.

Many reasons account for the Confederate defeat. Fighting on strange ground a long way from home played heavily on the troops. *Lee* exercised his command very loosely, giving too much responsibility to green corp commanders like *Hill* and *Ewell*. *Longstreet* was slow and *Stuart* was even slower. The blame falls in many places.

Whoever or whatever the reasons, the end result was the same. The *Army of Northern Virginia* was in full retreat back to Virginia. *Imboden's* cavalry and the wagons took the route through the Cashtown pass and *Lee* led the army through Fairfield to Hagerstown. From Hagerstown, the march led south to the Potomac River.

The heavy rains of the previous week had left the Potomac in flood stage. Fording was impossible and raiding Union cavalry had destroyed the pontoon bridges at Williamsport. *Lee* ordered a defensive line dug and waited for an assault by Meade.

But Meade's cautious attitude prevailed long after the battle. Beyond cavalry feints, Meade ordered no offensive action by his corps, even when odds were greatly in their favor. Despite his 80,000 troops against 50,000 of *Lee's*, Meade delayed long enough for *Lee* to throw a pontoon bridge over the river at Falling Waters and get his army safely across into Virginia. The escape had been made.

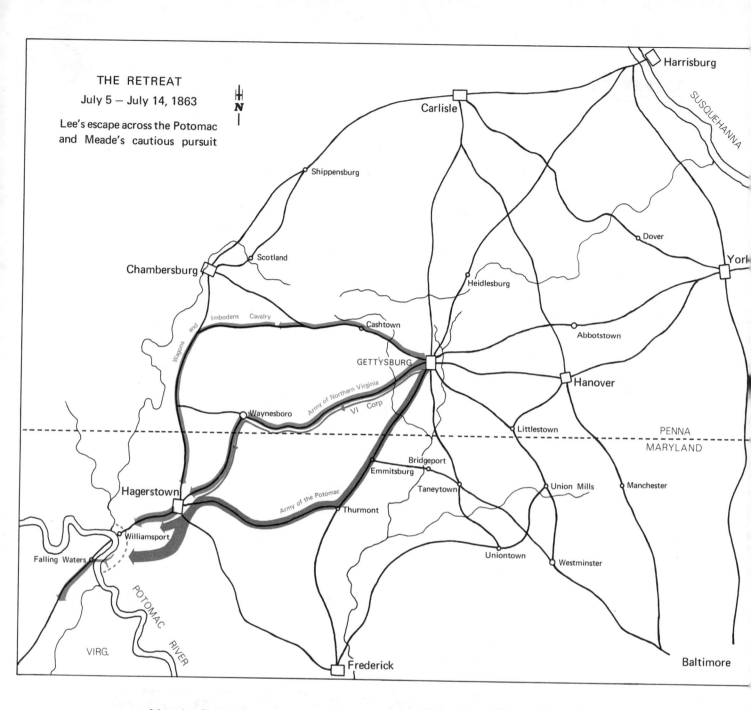

THE RETREAT

July 5 – July 14, 1863

Lee's escape across the Potomac and Meade's cautious pursuit

Meade finally ordered an attack against the rear guard which resulted in over 2,000 Confederate casualties, including the death of General *James Pettigrew*. The officer who started the battle also played out its final scene.

The Gettysburg campaign, lasting forty-two days from June 3 until July 14, 1863, was responsible for over 52,000 casualties, everyone an American.

The war went on for another two years with destruction of property and destruction of lives. In later battles, Gettysburg's casualty list seemed low by comparison. But a battle's importance cannot be measured in lives. It must be measured by what effect their deaths had on the eventual outcome of the war. At Gettysburg, a bold plan was met by a desperate defense, and both knew that the one who lost would also lose the war.

CASUALTIES

Although the list of casualties at the Battle of Gettysburg was not the largest of the war, it was one of the most severe. The losses on both sides were nearly equal, and enormous for the number of combatants engaged.

The magnitude and closeness of action produced a rather large number of high ranking officers as casualties and many individual units had casualties almost to the point of annihilation.

The Confederates lost 18 Generals, 5 of whom were killed, 11 were wounded, and 2 captured. The Union lost 15 General officers, 3 of whom were killed, 11 wounded, and 1 captured. In actual count, the amount of brigade commanders and above who fell were about the same. The fact that the Union Army was slow on promotions accounts for their lower number of Generals. As brigade commanders, the Union lost 4 Colonels killed and 4 wounded. The Confederates lost 1 Colonel killed leading a brigade.

The fighting on July 1 was fierce but often local. General *Heth* reported that he lost 40% of his division in the first 25 minutes of combat, but the *26th North Carolina* of this division had 76% casualties. One company of this regiment lost 86 out of 87 men who went into action. *Heth's* Division, which numbered over 7,000 men suffered nearly 3,000 killed, wounded, or missing.

The front line on McPherson's Ridge was equally **rough** on the Union. The tough Iron Brigade suffered 61% casualties or 1,153 out of 1,883 engaged. Stone's Brigade lost 66% but the 150th Pennsylvania of this brigade lost nearly 75%. Biddle's Brigade lost over 70% of his effectives. In the Union I Corps, over 6,000 out of 8,200 engaged fell, a loss of over 70%. For an entire Corps, this was an extremely high percentage.

Unusual situations developed too. The 107th Pennsylvania of Paul's Brigade captured more prisoners that the regiment itself numbered. The 16th Maine, also of Paul's Brigade, acting as rear guard on the Mummasburg Road, suffered 11 killed, 62 wounded and 159 captured out of 275. General Robinson had two horses shot from under him and General Baxter lost his entire staff in the bloody fight on the I Corps right flank.

General *Heth* suffered a severe head wound when a minie' ball circled his hat inside the band. The fact that the hat was too large saved his life. Union General Schimmelpfennig, cut off during the XI Corps retreat, hid for two days under a woodpile to avoid capture.

The Confederate force attacking Culp's Hill numbered 36 regiments, mostly from *Johnson's* Division. Their losses were 458 killed, 2,338 wounded and 622 missing or captured. Their Union opponents, mostly from the XII Corps, put only 28 regiments on the field. Their losses were 204 killed, 810 wounded and 67 missing or captured. This was less than a third of the Confederate losses.

Pickett's Division numbered nearly 4500 men before its part in the great assault on July 3. Their losses were 232 killed, 1,157 wounded, and 1,499 missing or captured. This was relatively few casualties for such a bold attack.

The loss of high ranking officers at Gettysburg hurt both sides that were already lacking in adequate leadership. The Union perhaps suffered the greatest with the loss of General Reynolds. The following list shows the high amount of officers lost:

ARMY OF THE POTOMAC

ARMY OF NORTHERN VIRGINIA

Corps Commanders:

Maj Gen Reynolds — Killed

Maj Gen Sickles — Wounded (Lost leg)

Maj Gen Hancock — Wounded

None

Division Commanders:

Brig Gen Rowley — Wounded

Brig Gen Gibbons — Wounded

Brig Gen Barlow — Wounded

Maj Gen Doubleday — Wounded

Maj Gen Pender — Killed

Maj Gen Hood — Wounded

Maj Gen Heth — Wounded

Maj Gen Trimble — Wounded/Captured

Brigade Commanders:

Brig Gen Weed — Killed

Brig Gen Farnsworth — Killed

Colonel Zook — Killed

Colonel Cross — Killed

Colonel Willard — Killed

Colonel Vincent — Killed

Brig Gen Graham — Wounded/Captured

Brig Gen Webb — Wounded

Brig Gen Paul — Wounded

Brig Gen Stannard — Wounded

Colonel Biddle — Wounded

Colonel Stone — Wounded

Colonel Brooke — Wounded

Colonel Smyth — Wounded

Brig Gen Garnett — Killed

Brig Gen Armistead — Killed

Brig Gen Barksdale — Killed

Brig Gen Semmes — Killed

Colonel Avery — Killed

Brig Gen Kemper — Wounded

Brig Gen Scales — Wounded

Brig Gen Anderson — Wounded

Brig Gen Pettigrew — Wounded

Brig Gen Posey — Wounded

Brig Gen Robertson — Wounded

Brig Gen Jones — Wounded

Brig Gen Hampton — Wounded

Brig Gen Jenkins — Wounded

Brig Gen Jenkins — Wounded

Others:

Maj Gen Butterfield — Wounded

Maj Gen Warren — Wounded

70

Of the states represented in the Union Army, many suffered high losses. Pennsylvania had the largest number present, nearly 35,000 men, but they ranked second in losses. The list of states losing 1,000 or more is as follows:

New York	6,746
Penna.	5,891
Mass.	1,537
U.S. Regulars	1,374
Ohio	1,271
Michigan	1,111
Maine	1,027

The following table lists the casualties by Corps for the Union and Confederate forces during the three day battle.

Union		Confederate	
I Corps	6,059	I Corps	7,576
II Corps	4,369	II Corps	5,937
III Corps	4,211	III Corps	6,935
V Corps	2,187	Cav Corps	240
VI Corps	242		
XI Corps	3,801		20,688
XII Corps	1,082		
Cav Corps	852		
Art Res	242	Total loss in the Union Army was 27%
	23,045	Total loss in the Confederate Army was 30%

Total losses in the Union Army were as follows:

Killed	Wounded	Missing/Captured	Total
3,155	14,525	5,365	23,045

Confederate casuality records were seldom accurate and often never reported by regiments. A reasonably accurate breakdown is as follows:

Killed	Wounded	Missing/Captured	Total
2,632	12,809	5,247	20,688

GLOSSARY

Artillery Battery   Six (north) or four (south) guns operating as a combined unit.

Artillery Battalion or Brigade   Large artillery unit composed of five to seven artillery batteries.

Artillery Reserve   Artillery batteries not assigned to combat units, rather, kept at one central point to allow quick, massive deployment.

Artillery Section   A two gun unit of an artillery battery.

Bivouac   Encampment for the night.

Breastworks   An embankment of earth, rocks, rails or trees to provide protection for an infantry line.

Breech-Loader   Type of cannon or rifle loaded from the rear of the barrel.

Brigade   Military unit composed of three to six regiments under a Brigader General or senior Colonel.

Canister   A thin metal can containing about 25 iron or lead balls, used by artillery against close infantry.

Carbine   Breech-loading rifle, usually carried by the cavalry because of its small size and ease of loading.

Case Shot   Hollow shell filled with 75 balls and a bursting charge. Fuses were cut to explode over infantry.

Caisson   A two wheeled vehicle used to carry ammunition (2 chests) for an artillery piece.

Cavalry   Mounted forces used to raid, scout, and protect flanks and rear areas of the army.

Colors   Flags of a regiment or brigade carried into battle at the head of the attacking line. Also used as a rallying point if the unit gets dispersed.

Company   Small military unit composed of 50 — 100 men. Several companies formed a regiment.

Corps   Largest military unit composed of two or three divisions under a Major General (Union) or a Lieutenant General (Confederate). Corps are designated with roman numerals.

Division   Military unit composed of three to five brigades usually under a Major General or senior Brigadier General.

Flank   The ends of a battle line, vulnerable because no troops face that direction.

Horse Artillery   The artillery assigned to the cavalry corps.

Infantry   The foot soldier.

Limber   A two wheeled vehicle coupled with the caisson. The Limber also carried one ammunition chest.

Lunett   Half-circle embankment of earth thrown up to protect a piece of artillery.

Minie' Ball   A rifle ball, hollow at the base and fitted with a plug that expands to fit the rifling by the force of the exploding powder.

Muzzle-Loader   Type of cannon or rifle loaded by pushing the shell down the barrel.

Pickets   A group of soldiers deployed at outposts.

Rally   Reforming of a unit after an attack or retreat.

Regiment   A military unit composed of 100 to 800 men commanded by a Colonel. Regiments at full strength were 1,000 men, but two years of war had reduced many to mere fractions.

Rifled Bore   Bore of a cannon with spiral grooves cut into it to make the shell spin upon leaving the barrel. Improved accuracy resulted.

Shell   Hollow iron shells filled with powder. Fuses were cut to explode among enemy positions.

Signal Corps   The branch of military service that deals with communications.

Skirmish line   A thin line of troops deployed in front of a fixed line or marching column to warn of an attack.

Smooth Bore   Bore of a cannon with smooth sides, resulting in less accuracy.

Solid Shot   A solid iron round of ammunition.

Spiking   Ramming a metal rod in the vent-hole of a cannon and bending it inside, rendering it useless unless rebored.

Swab   A long ram-rod tipped with padding, used to clean and cool cannon barrels.

Trains   Wagons carrying supplies and ammunition that followed the army. Each Corps had its own trains, plus the Commissary, Ordnance, Medical and Quatermaster trains of the army.

Volley   The firing in unision of a company or regiment.